# Gandy Dancer

*A student-led literary magazine of the State University of New York*

Issue 14.1 | Fall 2025

**gandy dancer** /ˈɡan dē ˌdans ər/ *noun*
**1.** a laborer in a railroad section gang that lays and maintains track. Origin: early 20th century: of unknown origin.

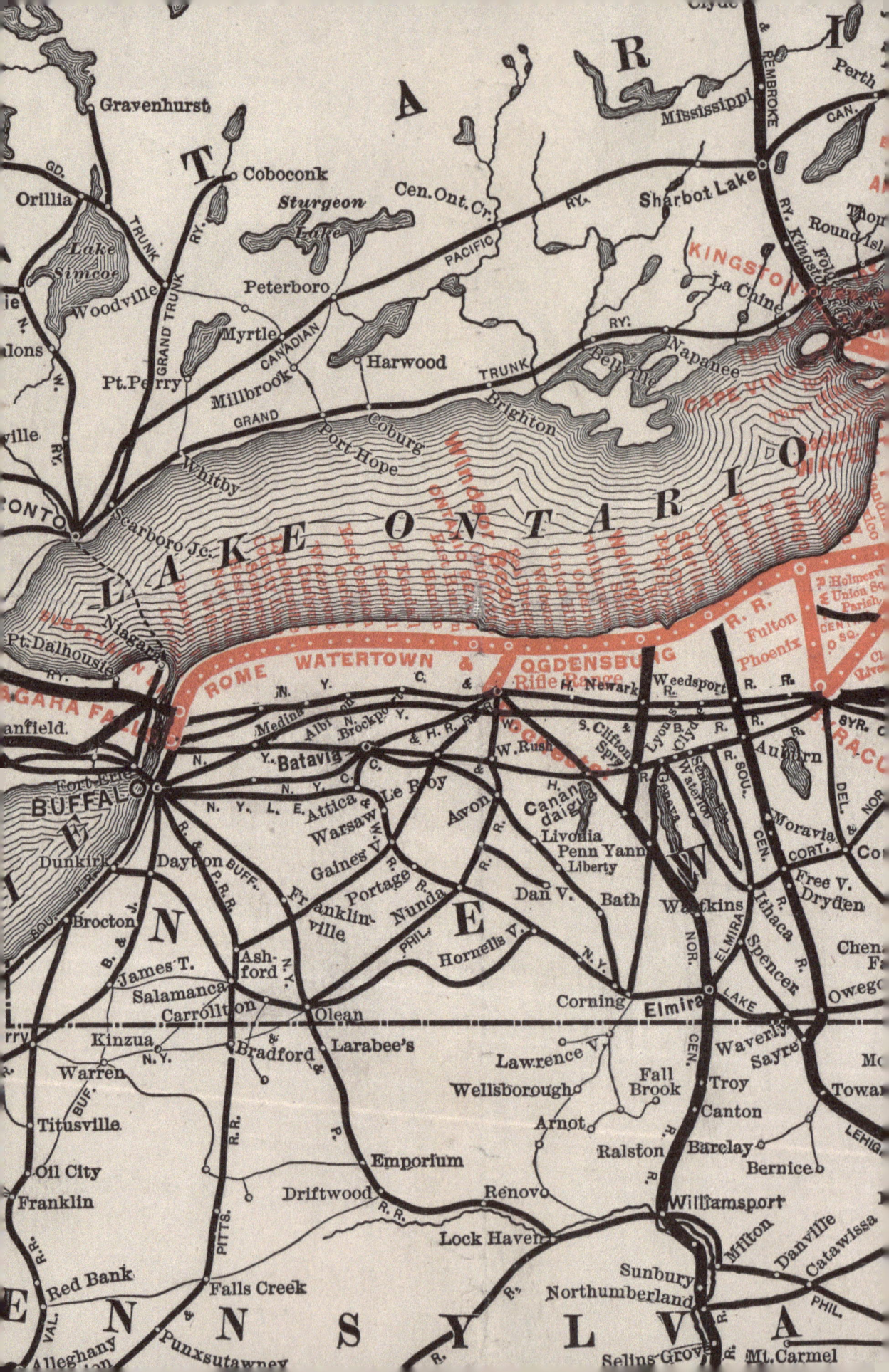

**gandy dancer** /ˈgan dē ˌdans ər/ *noun* **1.** a laborer in a railroad section gang that lays and maintains track. Origin: early 20th century: of unknown origin.

We've titled our journal *Gandy Dancer* after the slang term for the railroad workers who laid and maintained the railroad tracks before the advent of machines to do this work. Most theories suggest that this term arose from the dance-like movements of the workers, as they pounded and lifted to keep tracks aligned. This was grueling work, which required the gandy dancers to endure heat and cold, rain and snow. Like the gandy dancers, writers and artists arrange and rearrange, adjust and polish to create something that allows others passage. We invite submissions that forge connections between people and places and, like the railroad, bring news of the world.

*Gandy Dancer* is published biannually in the spring and fall by the State University of New York College at Geneseo. Issues of Gandy Dancer are freely available for view or download from gandydancer.org, and print copies are available for purchase. Special thanks to the College at Geneseo's Department of English and Creative Writing and Milne Library for their support of this publication.

ISSN: 2326-439X

ISBN (THIS ISSUE): 978-1-956862-19-5

We publish writing and visual art by current students and alumni of the State University of New York (SUNY) campuses only.

Our Postscript section features work by SUNY alumni. We welcome nominations from faculty and students as well as direct submissions from alumni themselves. Faculty can email Rachel Hall, faculty advisor, at hall@geneseo.edu with the name and email address for the alum they wish to nominate, and alums can submit through our website. Both nominations and direct submissions should indicate which SUNY the writer attended, provide a graduation date, and the name and email of a faculty member we can contact for confirmation.

We use Submittable to manage submissions and the editorial process. Prospective authors can submit at gandydancer.submittable.com/submit. Please use your SUNY email address for your user account and all correspondence.

*Gandy Dancer* will accept up to three submissions from an author at a time.

> FICTION: We accept submissions up to 25 pages. Stories must be double-spaced. We are unlikely to accept genre or fan-fiction.
>
> CREATIVE NONFICTION: We accept submissions up to 25 pages. CNF must be double-spaced.
>
> POETRY: Three to five poems equal one submission. Poems must be submitted as a single document. Format as you would like to see them in print. Our text columns are generally 4.5 inches wide, at 11pt font.
>
> VISUAL ART: We accept submissions of art—especially photos, drawings, and paintings—in the file formats jpeg, tiff, and png. Submitted images should have a minimum resolution of 300 dpi and be at least 5 inches wide. Please include work titles and mediums in your submissions.

Please visit us at www.gandydancer.org, or scan the qr code below.

Questions or comments? Send us an email at gandydancer@geneseo.edu

GENESEO | Milne Library

|                         |                                                                                                                    |
| ----------------------: | :----------------------------------------------------------------------------------------------------------------- |
|     *Managing Editors*  | Sonia Horowitz, Paige Loucks                                                                                       |
|  *Production Assistant* | Nina Avallone-Serra                                                                                                |
|            *CNF Editor* | Madelyn Perry                                                                                                      |
|        *Fiction Editor* | Sophia Imbriaco                                                                                                    |
|         *Poetry Editor* | Ella Singer, David Sweeney                                                                                         |
|            *Art Editor* | Casey Dapshi                                                                                                       |
|           *CNF Readers* | Abigail Axton, Nat Baron, Kayla Clark, Allie Konsevitch, Emily Sneider, Adanna Wolf                                |
|       *Fiction Readers* | Hannah Anagnostakos, Ryan Eck, Julia Gartley, Daisy Sheldon, Aubrey Stout Peters, Jack Towns                       |
|        *Poetry Readers* | Hailey Bilby, Taya Markham, Regan Russell, Alex Seney                                                              |
|       *Faculty Advisor* | Rachel Hall                                                                                                        |
|    *Production Advisor* | Allison Brown                                                                                                      |
| *Social Media Manager*  | Liberty Dodds                                                                                                      |
|      *Advisory Editors* | Sonya Bilocerkowycz, Dan DeZarn, Kristen Gentry, Lucia LoTempio, Mehdi Okasi (Purchase), Michael Sheehan (Fredonia), Lytton Smith, Kathryn Waring |

*Founding Editors: Emily Webb, Samantha Hochheimer, Emily Withers, Stephon Lawrence, Megan Nolan, D'Arcy Hearn, Jim Ryan, Megan Cicolello, Andrea Springer, Bibi Lewis, Jennie Conway, Suraj Uttamchandani*

*Special thanks to: the Parry family and Sarah Cedeño*

# Dear Readers,

In our roles as managing editors and production assistant, our hope was to create a space where we felt comfortable building close relationships with each other, our peers, and you—the reader—bolstering the broader creative community that *Gandy Dancer* has embodied for thirteen years. As the experiences we get from this class are inextricably linked to the world around us, we felt it was crucial in times like these to build strong bonds with each other that reflected the relationships and conversations we want to have outside of Welles 216. We chose to do this by way of genre group bonding—going out to coffee and having movie nights—with the goal of getting to know each other more intimately. As we were reviewing pieces this semester, we realized that our contributors were occupied with similar questions about their connections to place, family, self, and even our political climate. And now, we share them with you.

Lori Yamond's braided essay "The Womb Shaped Fruit" investigates the intricate ties that bind us to the earth, to our mothers, and to ourselves. Balancing individual threads that discuss the role of the fig in the lifespan of the wasps it hosts and the struggle to maintain individuality in the midst of motherhood, Yamond asks us to confront ourselves: "We wish to turn a blind eye to the pain ravaging the woman whose motherhood has labeled her as resilient. Maybe this blind eye has given us the courage to be the ones to cause the ravaging pain…" By exploring the unique harm borne by those, human and otherwise, who create and sustain life, Yamond prompts a deeper conversation about our relationship to an environment in flux.

The work published here plunges deeper into the typical connections people have and breaks them down piece by piece, revealing why we build relationships in the first place. For example, in Kira Hook's short story "Looking Down From Parliament Hill," the narrator reflects on her miscarriage and how it affects her relationship with herself, with what was lost, and the partner with whom she shares this lost child. Perhaps in connection with Sylvia Plath's poem, "Parliament Hill Fields," which was written a week after Plath's miscarriage, Hook places us in the narrator's thoughts as "she swallows the name she gave to tissue, mucus, and bloody cells." The image of blood and pieces of the body highlight the dissonance and desire for connection the narrator has to what was lost. We even see her recognize her feelings about her husband in the moment and how "her countenance is fractured under her husband's gaze." Hook brings this moment to life in just one page, and in this brevity, she reveals something profound about our narrator and her conception of her loss, underscoring the raw reality of grief and the complex reasons we seek connection in such difficult times.

The art included here also examines the need for relationships and connection, as well as the many different places one might find it. Michaela Chittenden's "The American Dream" transports us to a fifties-style American living room, where a family is watching Elvis performing on the television. The smile of the woman sitting on the floor gives us a sense of hope and that even something as simple as watching TV can bring a whole world together. Natalie Vazquez-Martinez's colorful self portraits, playing with mediums as varied as oil on canvas in "Me" and "Moi," and painted wood blocks assembling a still more abstract face, provide a sense of the strange and everchanging nature of one's relationship to self.

This issue doesn't just examine personal and interpersonal relationships; it also considers dynamics of authority and how they affect our lives as a whole. In the midst of the current administration, the longest government shutdown in U.S. history, and countless headlines regarding our political landscape, individuals have had to reassess their relationship with the government, their communities, and the planet. The poets in this issue have put themselves in the epicenter of current events, both in the world and their own backyards, to deliver a reminder of our place in it all. Michael Crowley's poem "Subtropic" explores climate change through memories of enjoying native fruits in New York that will no longer thrive in the state's new "humid subtropical climate." Monty Cooke's "Zainab Abu Halib" tells of five-month-old Zainab Abu Halib, a Palestinian "baby who will never be a child" who starved to death in Gaza. In "My Method to Slightly Mitigate the Harm of Wealth Inequality" Owen Penhollow brilliantly, and comedically, outlines how the 1% could *really* benefit the rest of us by naming buildings after "the most heinous rich person" so we might get a discount out of it.

We want this issue to serve as a place where you can see and find yourself. As the new stewards of the magazine, we came into our roles seeing how the growing shadow of censorship has seeped into our everyday lives, building anxiety over a possible dark future for our journal and others like it. Because of this, and in addition to recent cuts to education and the arts, we knew it was even more integral to continue to allow *Gandy Dancer* to be a place where all voices, experiences, and experiments can find a permanent and unwavering home. "Elinguation" by Monty Cooke stands as a pillar, a reminder that "The tongue is mightier than the sword (…) if you know what you fight for." It's a scary world out there, full of adversity that threatens to consume us. However, this journal affirms that even in the face of difficult dynamics, it is crucial to find a safe space to confront those issues—this is ours. We hope you love 14.1 as much as we do, and maybe even find a sense of home in it too. We can't wait to see you again next semester.

Always in your corner,<br>
Nina Avallone-Serra, Sonia Horowitz, and Paige Loucks

# Table of Contents

Dearest Readers   *vii*

**FICTION**

Kira Hook
   *Looking Down from Parliament Hill*   4

Noah Banas
   *His Own Eyes*   16

Katerina Ronconi
   *Finertipped in Wait*   53

Stephen Piazza
   *Confessions*   60

**CREATIVE NONFICTION**

Archer Maduro
   *Old Haunts*   22

Lori Yamond
   *The Womb Shaped Fruit*   80

**POETRY**

Jenna Curtis
   *Naked*   1
   *Moribund*   3

Jasmeen Kaur
   *What Holds Me, What Roars in Me*   5
   *When You Forget Who You Are (addressed to younger me)*   8

Alyssa Dawson
   *Smelling Salts*   12

Abigail Halbert
   *Fringes of Photographs*   24

Dan Owen De Vera
   *Mother and the Monsters*   25

Giulyana Gamero
   *Hanabiko*   26

Sheila Verkaik
- *Things Big and Small (The Seed from Which I Grew)* .... 31
- *Cultuurschok: Hoe je Spreekt Nederkaans* .... 32

Buzz Kozak
- *Zero Food Waste* .... 36
- *40mg Omeprazole, Once Daily* .... 38
- *Reservoir* .... 40
- *My 4th Annual Birthday Political Fundraiser* .... 42

Sam Carrillo
- *Madrid* .... 47

Rey Davis
- *In the Face of Nothing Else* .... 52

Belle Elyse
- *malpractice* .... 58

Paulina Bargnesi
- *The Misfortune Family's Limerick* .... 67

Owen Penhollow
- *My Method to Slightly Mitigate the Harm of Wealth Inequality* .... 68

Ana Paul
- *Lemonpoem* .... 72
- *Lover's Poem* .... 74

Michael Crowley
- *Subtropic* .... 76
- *Beach Day* .... 78

Monty Cooke
- *Zainab Abu Halib* .... 90
- *Elinguation* .... 91

**ART**

Monica Hejaily
- *Truro* .... 11

Jade Maracic
- *Heavy Eyes* .... 21

Victoria Stiver
- *Soul Snippets (1)* — 23
- *Mold Study* — 70
- *I Know It Exists Because I Feel It With You* — 71

Caitlin Andrejova
- *i miss you* — 28
- *Alex* — 29
- *Loving Memory* — 30
- *Torment* — 93

Gabriella Ferri
- *Quetzalcoatl* — 33

Sawyer Taylor Ramsamooj
- *Guardian Angel* — 34
- *Riptide* — 44
- *how do you want me?* — 45

Max Flanigan
- *Trash* — 35
- *Horizon* — 46

Natalie Vazquez-Martinez
- *Self-Portrait* — 48
- *Me* — 49
- *Moi* — 50
- *Leslie* — 51

Michaela Chittenden
- *Bring Him Home* — 57
- *The American Dream* — 59

Shadae Walker
- *Maliboo (Little Brother)* — 75

Emma Eager
- *Heartland* — 79
- *Nervous Condition* — 87
- *Metamorphoses* — 88
- *Cavity* — 89

**BOOK REVIEW (UPDATE)**
Sarah N. Lawson
> *Portraits of Struggle: A Review of Amina Gautier's At-Risk*  93

**INTERVIEW**
Sonia Horowitz
> *Interview with Sarah Cedeño*  96

**POSTSCRIPT**
Jesse Curran
> *Partly Cloudy, Landscape at Cagnes,* "*Seagull Motif (Violet and Green)*"  101

**ABOUT THE AUTHORS (UPDATE)**  *107*

*Cover photo: Torment — Caitlin Andrejova*

# Gandy Dancer

JENNA CURTIS

# Naked

*Front Yard, 1996,* Lida Suchy

in the
front yard

                                                I have roots that stretch
                                                    into the hands of

the river
that flows
in between

                                                           our lips

roots
that strictly            binds                        our legs
                                                         together

Watch
my grievances
flow free as the
                 leaves
                        keep
                           falling
                                              into a hollow
                                              place of murk

The swarms
of mosquitoes
and gnats
                   clouding
my sight

                                                                    the thorn of
                                                                    performance

                                                itching
                                                                    at the bite
Feel my
branches
break underneath
your
fingertips                                      I am

                                                                    naked

                                                                in the front yard.

JENNA CURTIS

# Moribund

at the point of death,
i made you up inside my head, relapses are
spinning as the tides are changing

the window is cracked open, cold air,
shoeprint made of your dust on the empty windowsill,
bleed myself dry at the point of death

heavy, heavy body, heavy mind, sinking
forgetting my to-do list, remembering the blurry body
spinning as the tides are changing

i made you up inside my head, i believe
the facade i created as you fled
cradled myself sick at the point of our death

sitting on the fire escape with the crackle of your lighter,
coughing out what we knew, burning my fingertips,
spinning as the            tides are changing

warm air flowing through my nostrils, a soundless home,
can't be tied to a "thing" or an "anyone," can't
bleed myself dry anymore, no longer at the point of death
            spinning free as the tides are always changing

KIRA HOOK

FICTION

# Looking Down From Parliament Hill

She watches as the red unravels and sprawls across the grimed toilet bowl. She holds the congealed clots that are too thick to slip through her fingers. Lights off, her knees are illuminated by the dim glow from the neighbor's window. Inside, she can see two silhouettes dripping into each other, pouring a black puddle of a shadow across her feet. The sound of their singing and laughter pierces through the humming water heater. They sound like hyenas to her. She holds the white strip under her legs as the stream trickles down her rug-burned wrist. It stings the sore opening. She wipes the blood from her hands and thighs and slips up her nylons. The flush rids it all. The stains on her hands loosen into pink, gentle water under the faucet. She leaves the bathroom still wet.

    He is draped across the couch, watching a rerun of a Yankees game from Thursday night. Her countenance is fractured under her husband's gaze. She smiles and wedges herself under his ungiving arm. The gin on his lips is enough to make her weak. Lily-livered, she holds him. He places his hand on her thin belly, mistaking his swelling palms for the soft tapping of a heartbeat. She moves it to her chest. He does not notice her strained breathing. The television screen flashes and swallows their tired expressions.

    Once he has fallen asleep, she returns to the bathroom. Water drips from the edge of the faucet. She flips on the light and peels the strip off the sticky counter. A single blue line is drawn across the paper. She swallows the name she gave to tissue, mucus, and bloody cells. She turns the light off and watches the flickering shadows in the window. They are quiet now, still and stalking.

JASMEEN KAUR

# What Holds Me, What Roars in Me

In the morning, I wear
my fuzzy sweater—
its softness reminds me
of when my grandfather
held my hand in Queens,
before we knew
we'd lose each other
to time's
quiet
migration.


A lotus biscuit melts on my tongue,
sweet like the perfume
my sister dabbed
on her wrist the day
she won her award.
I clapped loud—
louder than the ocean
we once ran toward, laughing,
salt clinging to our skin
like fries fresh from the bag.

I once saw a lion
stand in stillness—
not roaring,
just watching.
And I thought,
maybe courage isn't noise,
but knowing
when to stay.

I press the kara
to my wrist,
a cool circle of faith—
it grounds me
when I'm not sure
who I'm becoming.


Around my neck,
my gold necklace holds a locket
etched with the Khanda Sahib—
a quiet reminder
of who I am
when I forget.


At night, I help roll rotis
with my mom—
the dough soft between our palms,
her bangles clinking
like a quiet rhythm of care.


Sometimes I ask
the rice
as it runs
through my fingers,
what truly makes me happy?
It never answers.
But still,
I listen.

My other gold necklace
lies beside a crumpled note
from a friend back in Queens—
I almost threw it away.
It still smells like home.
I didn't know
how much I needed
small things
to stay.


I will do good in my classes,
I whisper,
watching the navy sky
turn maroon at dusk.


I will celebrate
my sisters' wins
like they are mine.


I will eat
something warm tonight–maybe chole, or dal–
and mean it
when I say
thank you.

JASMEEN KAUR

# When You Forget Who You Are

Dear one,
Keep the *kara* on your wrist,
even when it clinks too loud in classrooms
and makes you feel like you don't belong.
It is not just steel—
it is a circle that says you are never alone,
even on the days you feel most invisible.

Like the day you sat in the back row,
your lunch still warm in foil—*roti with mango achaar*—
while theirs came in paper bags with string cheese and Oreos.
No one said anything,
but you still folded the roti smaller,
hoping the smell wouldn't give you away.

When your voice shakes,
remember the sound of morning *paath*
coming from behind your parents' door—
the way it wraps around the house
like smoke, like a lullaby in reverse.
You didn't need to understand the words
for them to understand you.

Say thank you
to the warmth of *parshad*,
to the sweetness that sticks to your fingers
long after the prayer has ended.
Say thank you to the weight of your *Nani's chunni*
as she placed it on your head,
her touch saying more than any English word could.

You will want to leave parts of yourself behind.
Maybe your name, maybe your hair,
maybe the way you fold your hands
when you walk into a *Gurudwara*
and worry someone's watching.
Maybe even the little notebook you kept hidden,
where you wrote your name over and over
in bubble letters,
trying to make it smaller, more American,
less "too much."

But soft things survive too.
Your tears come from people
who crossed borders and buried their homes,
but still sang bedtime *shabads* at night.
Write your name in *Gurmukhi*,
even if your pen hesitates at every curve.
Even if no one else can read it.
It is still yours.
And that matters.

Let your hands smell like *cardamom* and *flour*,
your fingers stained orange from peeling *haldi*
with a butter knife on a steel plate—
the way you used to, sitting cross-legged
on the kitchen floor, humming without realizing.
The radio always too loud. Your braid too tight.
That quiet defiance was also a kind of faith.

Let yourself be touched by the world
and still walk through it whole.
And when it rains,
don't run.

Let it soak your *gutt*,
your doubts, your open palms.

Stand still like you're at the Golden Temple,
where even the sky feels like *ardaas*
falling soft over you,   -
a whisper that says:
you never had to be anything else
but this.

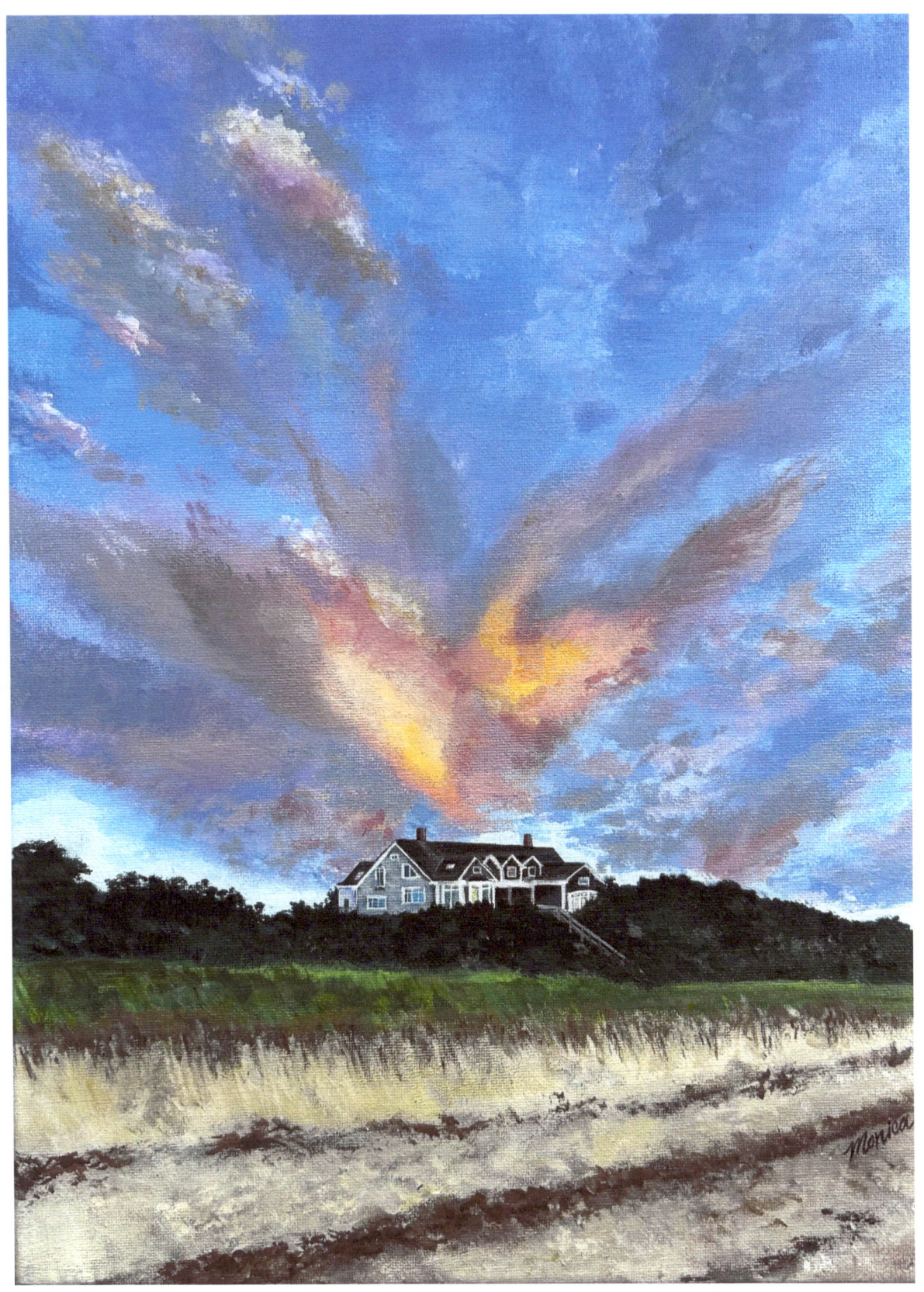

*Truro* (acrylic on canvas), Monica Hejaily

# Smelling Salts

### Home Scents
*March, 2025*

They say every home has a smell that its inhabitants are immune to—
too used to their own skin,
too complacent in their dust,
too wrapped up in living
to notice.

It is only when one goes on a long vacation—
the kind a meager poet's living cannot manage—
that the scent is apparent to those who make it.

Injustice!
I cry.

Because my dinner burns on the stovetop when I'm not paying attention

and my paint, pungent and opaque, runs freely from its tube when I'm focused

and I open my window when the daylight reeks of cigarettes and spring

and I burn sweet candles on passionate nights

and what is life if not a series of these things?

Yet still I cannot detect their cumulative stench—
my creation,
the only child I will ever be strong enough to care for,
the only figment I will ever have the right to,
my life,
my filth.

It's some kind of attack on the ordinary—

a curse that smells of humankind,

a smell to which I refuse to be immune

no matter how fast it dissipates.

## Him

*April, 2025*

Sometimes when I smell tobacco, I can't help but think of you,
or that horrible beer stench that always seems to find me on the weekends,
and it makes me angry.

I would like to believe myself immune to anger after all these years.
I would like to believe so,
but you wouldn't know.

One would think there would be an escape by now,
or at least I would—
it seems yours never came.

So I found one,
for me.

Yet still, every once and a while, I smell tobacco
and I can't help but think of you.

I think about the lake.
I think about the man who stood by it all those years, playing his instruments all at once,
and winning in the end.

I think about you, and the frozen custard we ate while we listened,
and the difference between frozen custard and ice cream.
Because there is one.
And, maybe there is one between then and now too—
just until I smell that terrible beer and I think of you.

I think about how your victory never came.
I thought for a while that I was supposed to be a part of it:
a trophy at least, a partner in crime at best.
But, I couldn't handle it—
when push came to shove, I laid down my weapons and ran.
And, you ran too,
but it seems escape never came for you.

## Home Scents (Part Two)

*April, 2025*

We lived in a brown brick apartment building
where the closets were nice enough and the kitchen often dirty.
It had a permanence to it.
It had a mother that did too,
even when nothing else felt that way.

Down the street lived a pink house
with lighter pink shutters and a nice looking glow in the young spring sun.
I noticed, but she didn't.

/

We lived in a building that I think was yellow,
but time leaves me unsure.
It had a leaky ceiling and a chipmunk in the wall.
It had a drunk, drunk man with a way of hiding it
from untrained noses.

Down the street sat a wooden store
owned by an older man and staffed by him too.
He gave me chocolate, and his door chimed when it opened.

/

We lived in a white house,
one that reeked of things past.
It had a thick carpet and
a couple of cats
(whom I miss dearly).

Down the street, everything has changed.

The pink house is white.

The man has gone to a foreign land.

Sometimes I feel like I have, too.

Until I smell the home scent,
pungent and varied,
and I remember
that I have never changed,
even when I wanted to,
even when I begged.

/

I drive by those houses every now and again,
because now we live in a gray one, and it's not the same.
The other ones are old to me now, but young to another,
I'm sure of it.
They have a permanence to them,
a foundation that doesn't quit,

and I haven't quit yet, either
(even when I wanted to,
even when I begged).

FICTION

NOAH BANAS

# His Own Eyes

He was the only person on the road. It was pitch black and the dim headlights of his old Corolla only let him see a few feet ahead at a time. The only other light was the digital clock that blinked on the dashboard—3:47 a.m. His eyes were half closed and covered by strings of thin greasy hair that crept out from under the brim of a red trucker hat. His clammy hands gripped the bottom of the wheel as he stared straight ahead into the tunnel of trees that lined the thin highway. He had woken up only half an hour earlier, and his head was still throbbing. He was getting used to the headaches—he hadn't slept well for weeks.

He tried to remember her face, as he often had. He had it mostly put together but not quite. He could picture her thin lips and the tiny mole in the corner of her nose, but couldn't recall the color of her eyes under all the mascara she wore that night. He remembered how her curly, dry hair felt on his fingers, but not what color it was. Just that it was dark. He never even learned her full name. He only knew her by Ellie. She didn't want to tell him her last name. Or maybe he forgot to ever ask. Her voice was the only thing still clear to him, as she had called just this morning—the call that woke him up. Their short conversation played over and over again in his head. For some reason he was glad that she had called him tonight. He wasn't sure she would. She'd shown no interest in talking to him after the suggestion he made the first time she called.

As he took the exit to the hospital his mind shifted to his parents; he had been thinking about them a lot recently. When he had gone home for the summer they barely talked to him. His father was an attorney who worked long hours at his firm and even longer hours in his home office. His mother was always home, but she would waste her days in front of the TV smoking

Newports. He rarely saw them interact with each other, and when he did it was usually when they teamed up to complain about his grades or lack of a job.

He knew their marriage wasn't a happy one. They were very young when they had him—his father had just started law school, and his mother was still in college. He didn't need anyone to tell him that he had been an accidental pregnancy. His parents had a shotgun wedding just six months before he was born, and his mother had dropped out of school.

During the summer he found an old photo album his parents had made to document the first year of his life. There were maybe nine or ten pictures in the book before it cut off, the rest of the pages blank. There was one of him in a stroller, another of his first birthday, his face covered in frosting. The rest looked almost identical—still images of him lying in his crib, except for one photo of him and his parents together in the hospital, right after he was born.

That tiny Polaroid haunted him. His parents stared blankly through the frame, both offering only the faintest of smiles, as he lay obliviously on his mother's lap, staring up at them with his big blue eyes. They looked scared. That only made him feel worse. He hadn't been able to talk to them at all about his situation with Ellie. He had no clue how they would react, and he was scared to find out. His parents never tried to connect with him. They kept on him about school, but other than that, everyone in the family kept to themselves.

His hands began to tremble as he pulled into the hospital complex. It was the only building for miles. The parking lot was surprisingly empty, and it was still pitch dark other than a few lights at the entrance. He sat in his parked car for a few minutes, completely still. He wanted nothing more than to leave—but he knew he'd never forgive himself if he wasn't there. Neither would Ellie. He didn't know if he cared what Ellie thought of him, but he still felt obligated to her. He didn't want to be a deadbeat. He considered himself a responsible person.

He thought back to the night he met Ellie in a bar a few miles from where he went to school. He remembered her telling him that she no longer spoke with her parents, that she had left home just weeks after graduating high school. He often fantasized about doing the same, but he knew he never could; his parents still paid for his school, his groceries, everything. He wondered if this was what attracted him to Ellie in the first place—she was independent, and didn't rely on anyone but herself.

He couldn't remember much else from the night they'd spent together. He remembered waking up in her small, grimy apartment tucked above a smoke shop. The whole room smelled like cigarettes. It reminded him of his mother. He left before Ellie even woke, crawling over piles of dirty laundry and scattered papers. He felt a little bad, but she was an attractive girl, and he was sure she had guys over all the time. Leaving wasn't anything personal.

It was two months later when he heard from her again. He didn't even know how she got his number. He remembers the whole experience like a dream, a surreal vision. He was in his friend's apartment, and when he stepped out to take the call he didn't come back. He must have talked to Ellie for hours before she hung up on him. He hadn't said anything to comfort her, to offer his support. She hadn't called since.

Eventually he just took a deep breath and got out of the car. He was so distracted he could barely feel the biting December winds. It was snowing for the first time that year, but he didn't notice. His feet stumbled beneath him as he made his way over to the big glass hospital doors. He made his way around the few people in the waiting room to a woman sitting at a round wooden desk at the center of the lobby. The woman sent him on his way to the maternity wing.

Ellie's room was labeled with a small slip of paper with her name on it. His heart dropped the second he saw her lying there. She looked nothing like the vague image that had been lingering in his mind; her skin was as pale as the hospital walls, and her dark curly hair was twisted into a careless, tangled bun. The crumpled hospital gown she wore clung tight to her damp skin and was covered in patches of sweat that had soaked through. There were empty beds lined up beside her, but the only other person in the room was an elderly nurse who was scribbling something on a clipboard.

Both women turned slowly toward him as he walked through the doorway, each offering a superficial smile.

"Is this him, Mom?" the nurse asked.

Ellie nodded.

The nurse walked over and grabbed him by the arm. Her smile was bigger now. "Give me one second, I'm gonna go make sure he's ready to say hello." She left the room, leaving him and Ellie by themselves.

"How are you feeling?" he asked, standing uncomfortably.

"I'm okay. It went pretty normal, I think. How are *you* feeling?" she half-laughed. "You probably look worse than I do."

He realized she was right. He felt his face burning and sweat dripping from every crevice on his body, "Uh…um…"

She laughed again, this time sounding annoyed. "It's okay. I did fine without you."

"It's not like you gave me much of a heads up."

"I told you seven months ago."

"You know what I mean."

She lost her smile and turned her head away. "I wanted to do it by myself. You would've stressed me out. You didn't even want—"

"I've tried to apologize for that. I didn't know how to react."

"You didn't know how *I* was going to react. You meant what you said." She looked angry, and he realized that she hadn't forgiven him.

"I'm glad you called me tonight," he said.

"You have a right," she responded.

He didn't like this answer. For some reason, he wanted her to want him there. He wanted her to appreciate his effort. He'd driven all this way. Their conversation was interrupted when the nurse knocked loudly on the door.

"Ok, Dad," she said. "You can come with me to the nursery."

He cringed. Being called "Dad" made him uncomfortable. Before he left the room, he exchanged one last glance with Ellie. Her face was still solemn, and he realized in that moment that her eyes were gray.

The nurse took him to a glass window that looked into a room filled with cribs and incubators, a handful occupied by infants. The room was brighter than the rest of the hospital; the walls were painted a light pink and covered by big stickers of flowers and clouds.

"He's that one right there," the nurse said, pointing to a crib in the center of the room.

He felt a knot in his stomach as he stared at the baby, who was wrapped up in a bright blue blanket, sleeping quietly. It didn't look how he thought it would; its puffy face was beating red, and its waxy skin glistened under the fluorescent lights.

"Did you wanna hold him?" the nurse asked.

He didn't really want to. He had never held a child before. But he reluctantly agreed, not wanting the nurse to think less of him.

They entered the nursery, and the nurse lifted up the baby and placed it into his arms. He held it awkwardly until the nurse shifted his position so that the baby's head lay on his forearm.

"I'll leave you two alone," the nurse said as she left the room.

This startled him. He didn't really want to be alone with the baby; he had never even interacted with one before. He held it for a few seconds before it woke and began to cry. He thought it was a terrible sound, a sharp pain that was jagged in his ears. He shushed it as he rocked back and forth. He was pretty sure that was how to get a baby to be quiet. He saw it in a movie once.

After a minute the baby did start to quiet down. Relief washed over him—he didn't want the other infants to wake and cause a scene. But he felt proud, too. The baby had already responded to him, in a way.

He stood in silence, in shock, staring at his son. It stared right back up at him with big blue eyes, eyes he recognized from that Polaroid of his family. For the first time that night, his breath slowed and he didn't feel the tightness in his chest. He was almost comfortable. He stood quietly in the room looking around, waiting for the nurse to come and take it back.

When the nurse did come back, she asked him politely to leave the nursery, insisting that the baby needed sleep. He handed the baby to the nurse and left the room. He heard it start to cry again as he walked away. To his own surprise, a part of him wanted to turn around and rock the baby back to sleep.

As he made his way through the long hospital hallways, he realized that he felt a bit more at ease than when he arrived. He had come seeking some sort of closure—but he realized that was impossible now. That was his child and he owed something to it, even if he didn't know what. When he got back to Ellie's room, he noticed a phone hanging on the wall just outside the door. He didn't even know if it was for public use, but he dialed his parents' home number anyway.

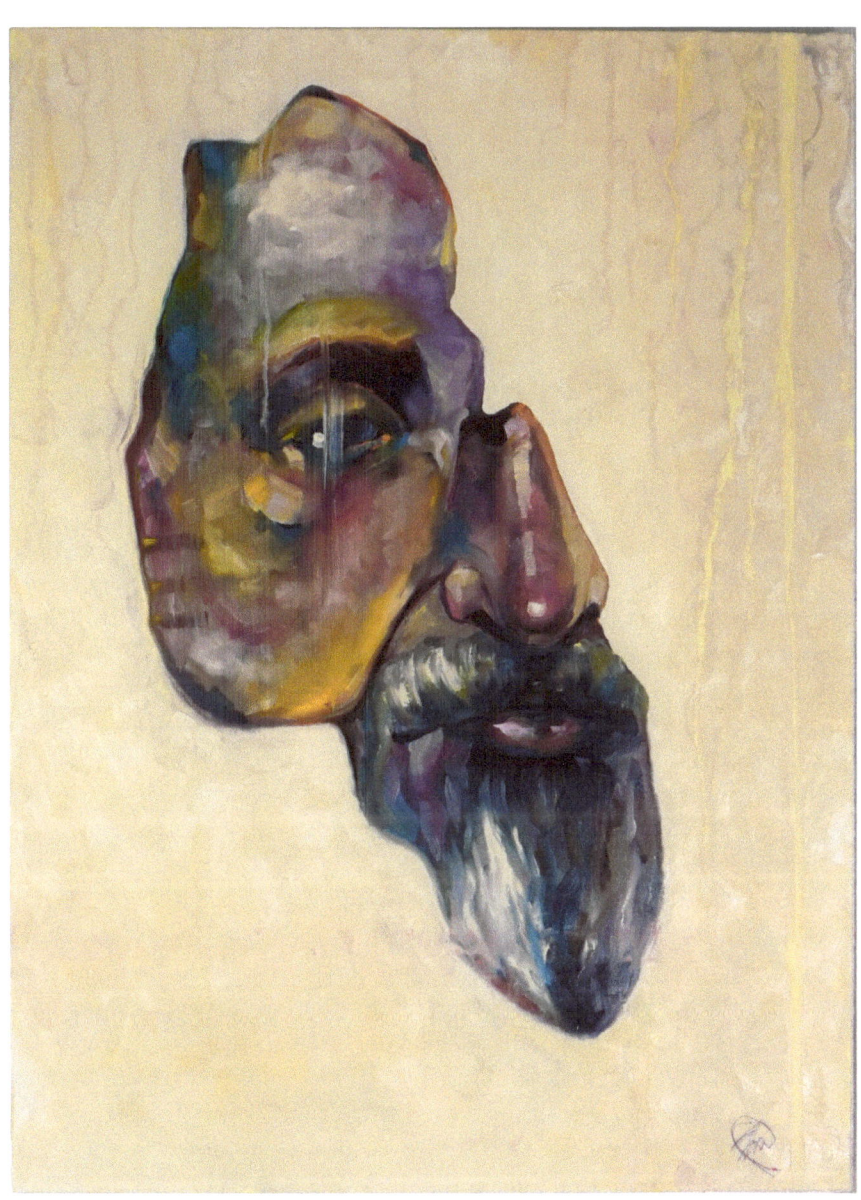

*Heavy Eyes* (oil on canvas), Jade Maracic

ARCHER MADURO                              CREATIVE NONFICTION

# Old Haunts

I'm back in my old haunt. I don't flinch when I stare down the peephole this time. When I double-check the door lock, which doesn't quite catch on the first try before bed, there's no triple-checking on an eyehole stuffed with wadded-up tissue.

I'm back in ~~my~~ our old haunt. The light stays on. A battery-powered wax candle becomes a cheap desk lamp becomes a fluorescent overhead bulb, lest a devoid, sallow-eyed figure find opportunity to stare from a dark corner. Wasted electricity beats wasting away.

I'm back in my old haunt. Stars are puttied to the popcorn ceiling where there weren't any before. (Technically, they're stuck to the walls—such beloved fire codes—but staring at a wall isn't as poetic at night as staring at the ceiling.) I turn my mattress sideways against the opposite wall, engulfed by the same sheets. But a washing machine cycle, or several thousand, works wonders. I change my detergent and fill the dryer with lavender sheep's wool, but scents don't cling the way shadows do. There's a new rug down the hallway, new lamps, and new (old) couches. If it all looks nothing alike, then it's hardly the same place at all.

I'm back in ~~my~~ our old haunt. *Exposure therapy is healthy*, I remind myself mid-lather. From my periphery, the folds of the polyethylene curtain shift just right, and I see your silhouette. The automated lights (in their convenient timing) flicker out. The showerhead, elbow-nudged from boiling lobster to boiler room, spills down and sizzles where skin and acid rain meet. My hair catches in the drain, creeps back up, and wraps around my toes. They tangle and tug until my knees hit the tile. In blind thrashes, I reach for the switch. Upon enlightenment, I'm greeted by toppled soap bottles and empty space. The grout stings my knees. The suds, my eyes. The phantom outline, everything else.

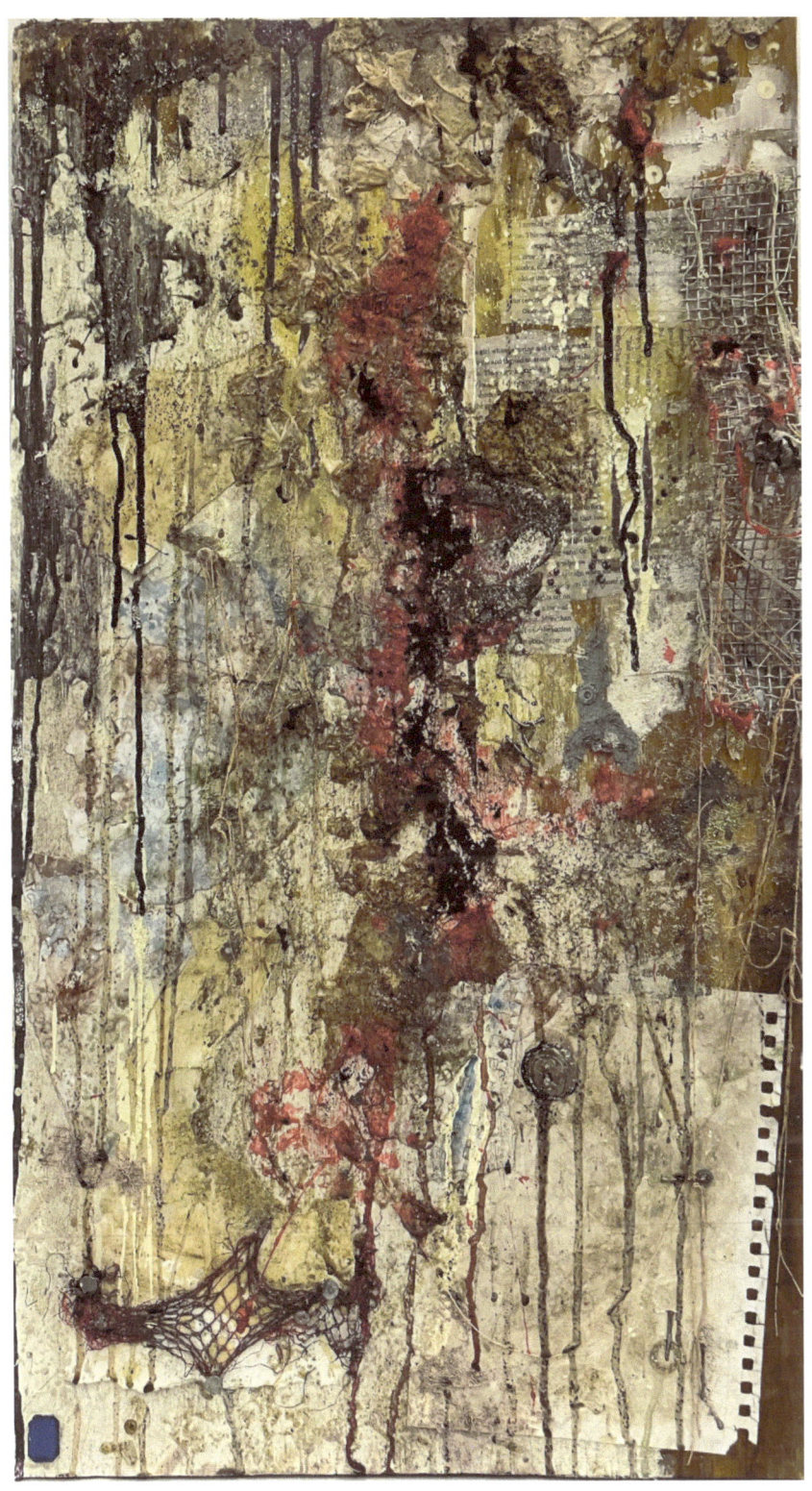

*Soul Snippets (1)* (acrylic and mixed media), Victoria Stiver

ABIGAIL HALBERT

# Fringes of Photographs

grey swirling clouds
lurk upon the
world's edges darkening
the chemically altered
page of summer day
blues and oranges
permeating the breath of the
gap-toothed girl bathed in
white
lilies and bleeding hearts
weighing down her feeble hands
callused paws of her
Father squeezing her waist
wine-red Mother—woman
clings to stained glasses
snuck in her purse
ignoring calls of LOOK HERE
scowling
stare transfixed
on the gap-toothed girl with her tight-lipped smile.

**DAN OWEN DE VERA**

# Mother and the Monsters

The hand is warm and frail, but the heart strong
and the hall is dark and deep, and colder.
As they step the night howls, its fierce reach long
for it lurks in silence, even bolder.
She leads slowly, one small step at a time,
e'er unbroken as she is wont to act.
Even with this hunched back now past its prime,
she leads carefully, to leave both intact.
Past the other bends and breaks, the hall ends,
and the child sits still, starting to whimper.
In the room she goes, to the dark she tends,
and, returning, curves her mouth to simpler.
The coast is clear. Nothing lurks in the deep.
Still, she joins the child. Together they sleep.

GIULYANA GAMERO

# hanabiko

sweet mother—
baby-made
finger paint display

carted out, presented whole
to mommy made

newspaper clippings.

fuzzy microphones jutted out
into the menagerie
but baby whimpers sound like song
and mommy made dialects.

eyes carved on window panes,
divisive—
isolated.

they dwell at home on concrete walls
instead of pastures that they're made in—

supposed to be: baby-made, baby arboretum
but mommy made award shows
trophies
and she will not concede them.

she will not concede them.

mommy made you
mommy::hero
fingers too big for speaking
mommy says them,
mommy sees them.

lynched on a tripod,
gored by the limelight,
eating whole and eaten raw:
digestible is the spectacle.

and, when you're gnawed completely,
totally to the bone,
they'll raise your skull on telecasts,
present you to the home

you knew
perhaps not what you wanted;
smartest chimp to ever live,
to ever be forgotten.

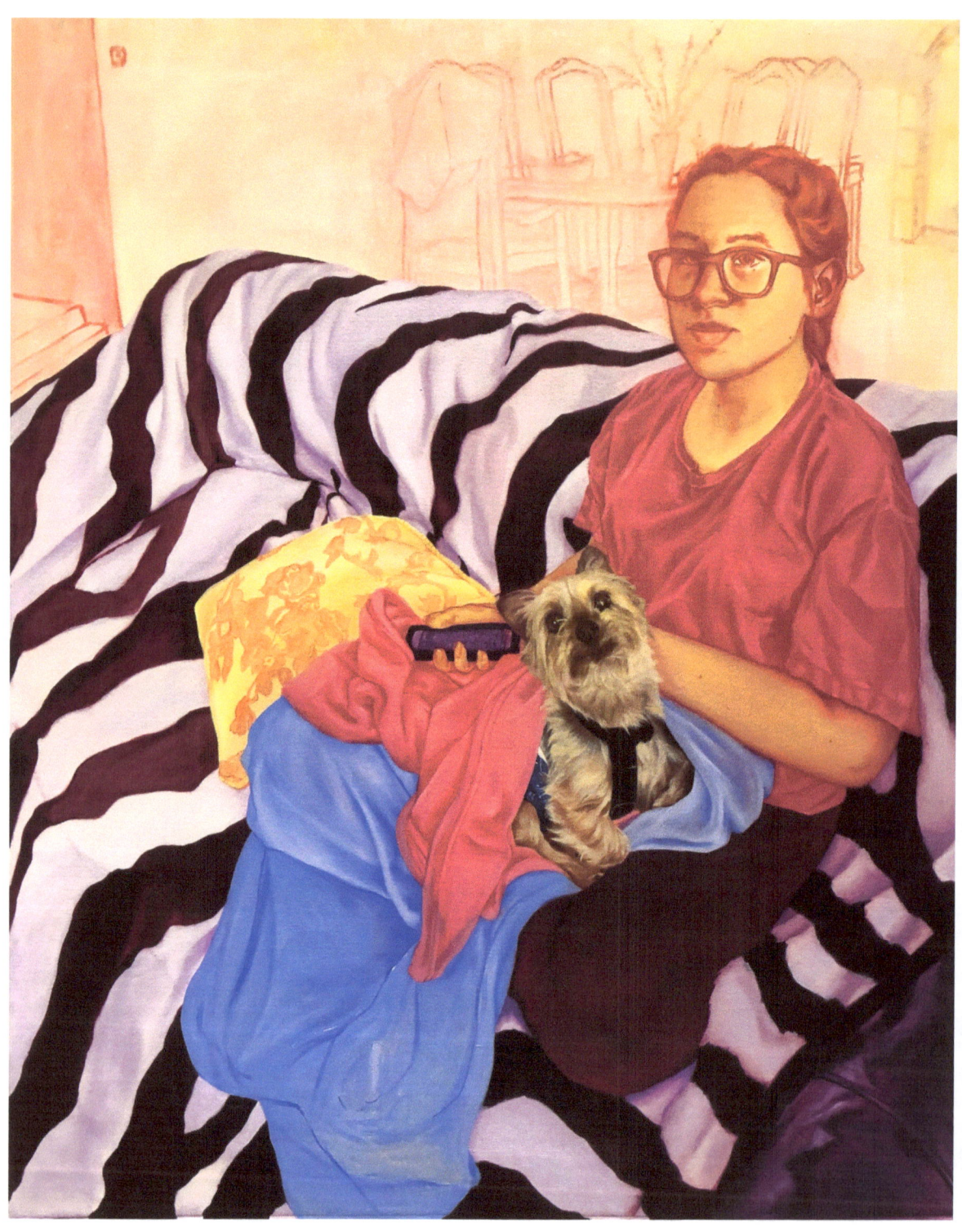

*i miss you* (oil on canvas), Caitlin Andrejova

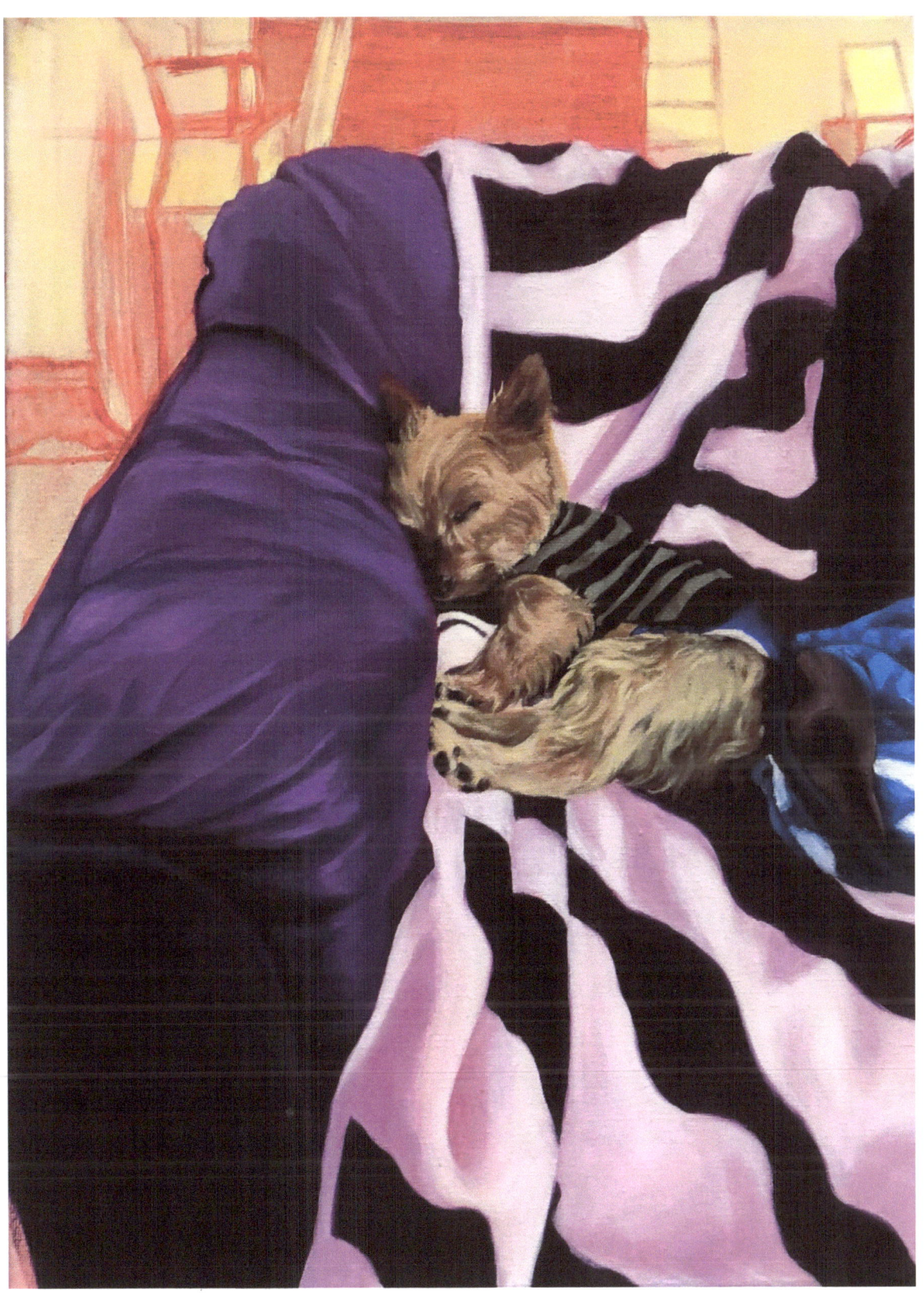

*Alex* (oil on canvas), Caitlin Andrejova

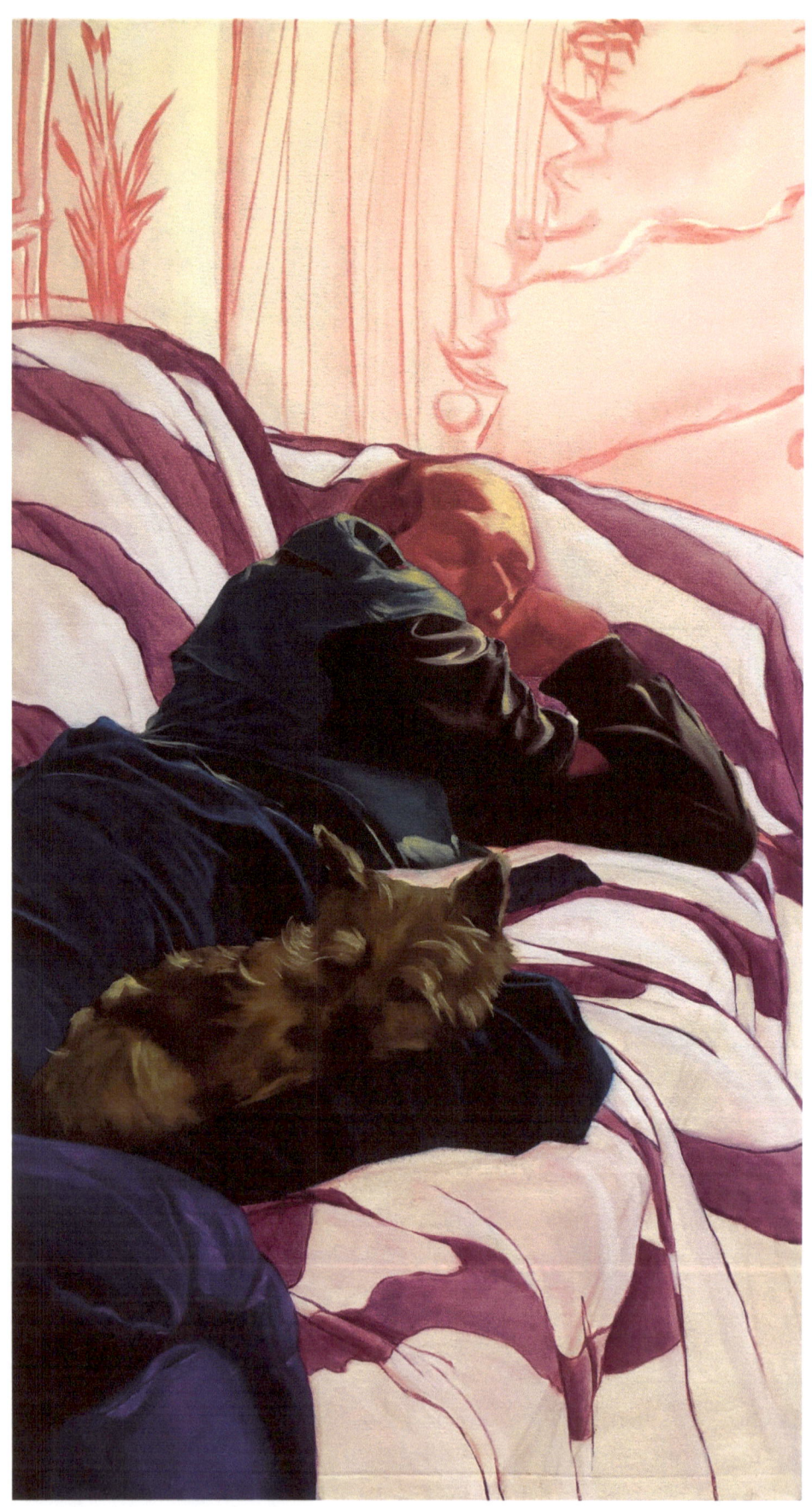

*Loving Memory* (oil on canvas), Caitlin Andrejova

**SHEILA VERKAIK**

# Things Big and Small (The Seed from Which I Grew):

Brownstones boiling beneath scorching sun,
Bring me back, to when this place belonged to me
A time when wheels thundered, a speed, never seen; when life had just begun
And Liberty bowed down, on hands and on knees, then offered the key

To all of humanity's finest creations: 1 dollar pizza slice gilded with grease
And boomboxes, blasted, through cracked car windows. Shattered by nothing. Rivaled only
By the shrieking of sirens, the seasonal Mister Softee, and the honking, of horns or of geese,
Which huddle on the shores of Harlem's meer, never lonely

Bounded by breadcrumbs and the bonds that they share
A beauty which most will never know. How lucky am I?
The inheritor of all this? This city, it bleeds you, sometimes without care
And yet, I still swear, I am the richest in the world. Big Apple of my eye

Raised from smog curtained skies, I click my heels thrice and I'm home
No matter how long nor how far I have flown, for I am the product of seeds, long sown.

**SHEILA VERKAIK**

# Cultuurschok: Hoe je Spreekt Nederkaans:

Pluizige dobbelstenen hangen aan de
achteruitkijkspiegel van een gele
schoolbus.
Een dankgeving kalkoen zit achterin.
You drive several miles to a Dutch grocery
store to find speciaal Gouda kaas,
het soort dat smelt als kindertijd op jouw tong
and reminds you of the cows on Opa's old farm.
On the drive back home
you can almost see the village windmills
turning in the distance,
but you know in your hart, that place is long gone.
Je kan nergens anders naartoe.

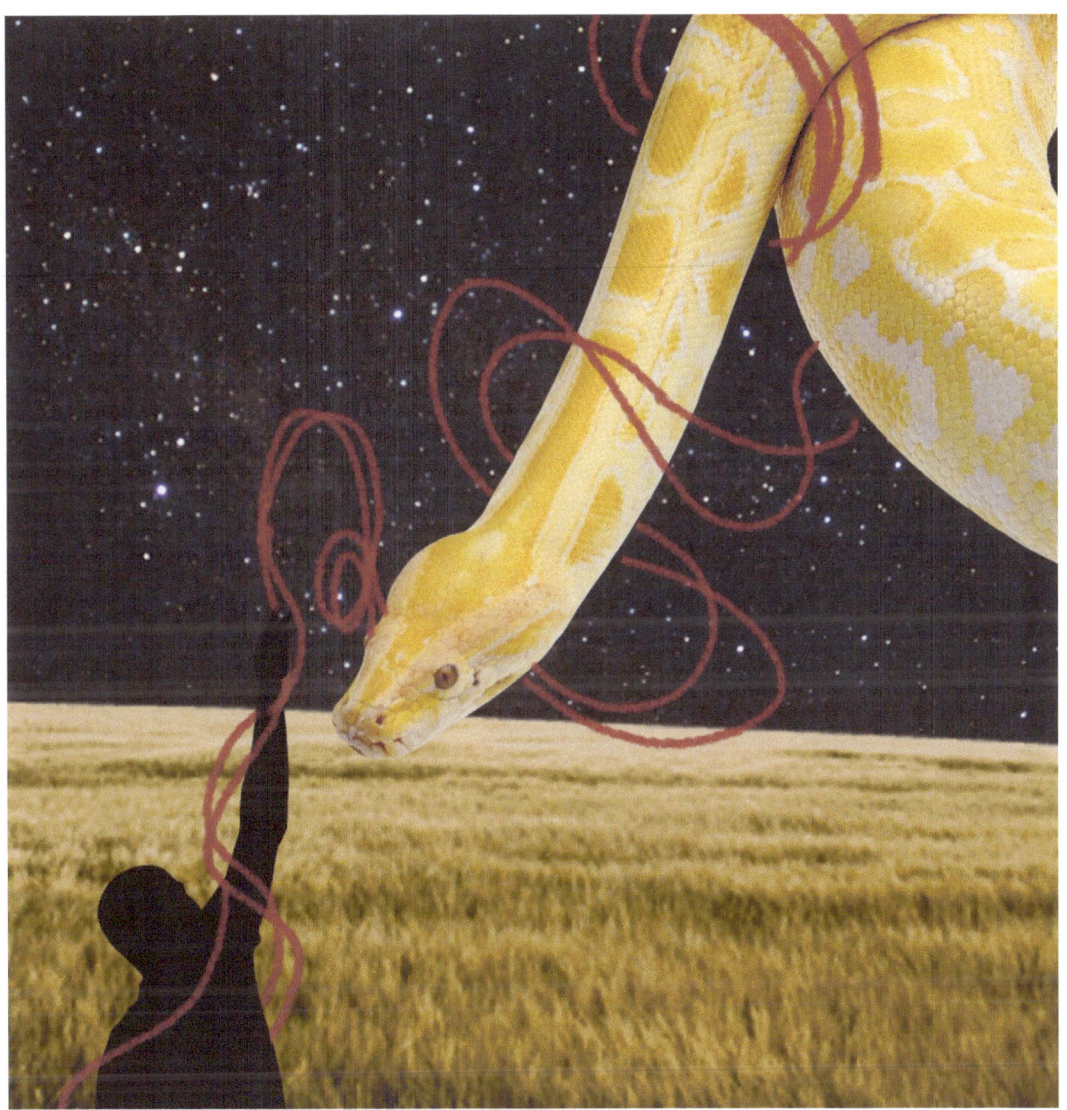

*Quetzalcoatl* (digital collage), Gabriella Ferri

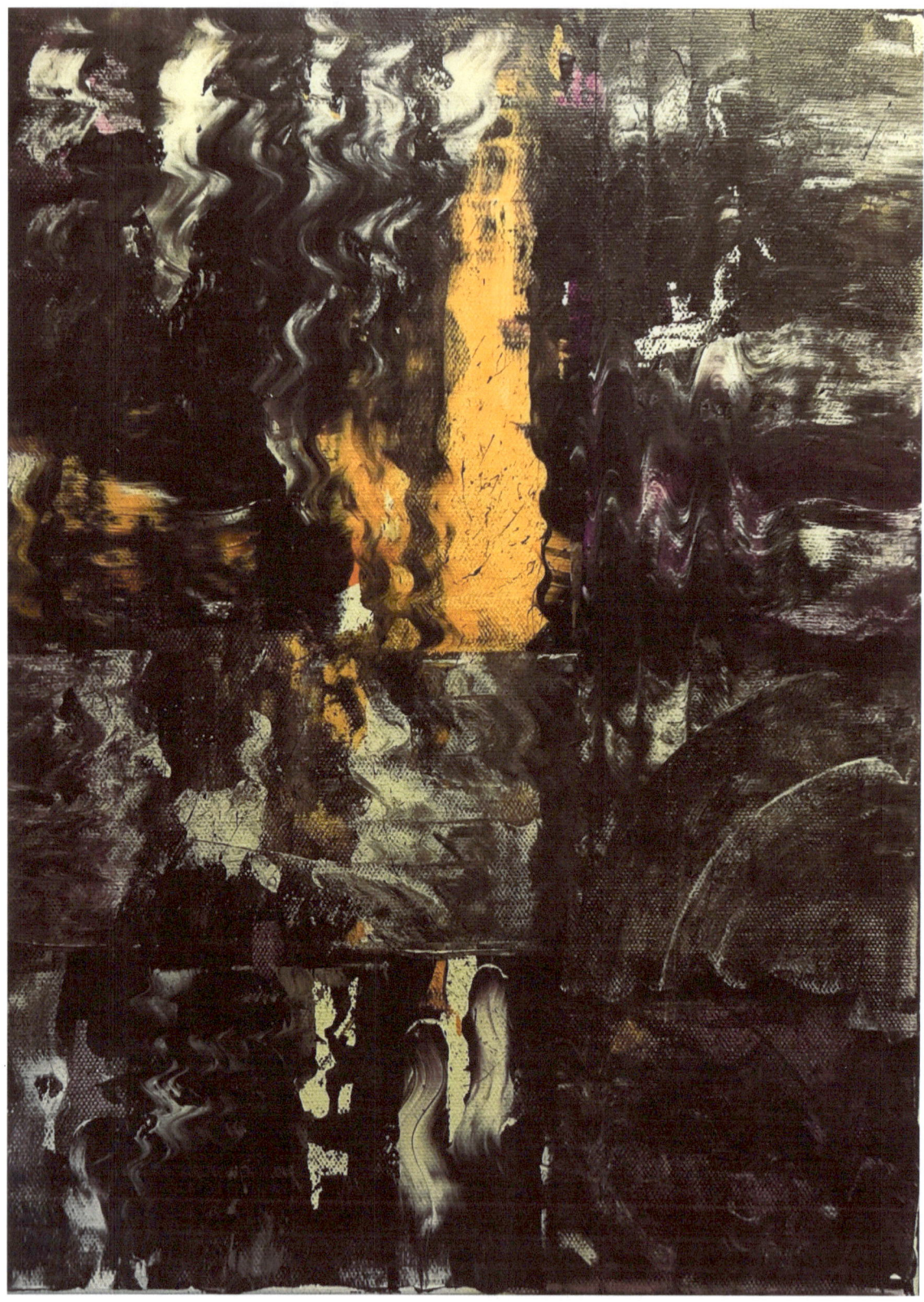

*Guardian Angel* (acrylic and ink on canvas), Sawyer Taylor Ramsamooj

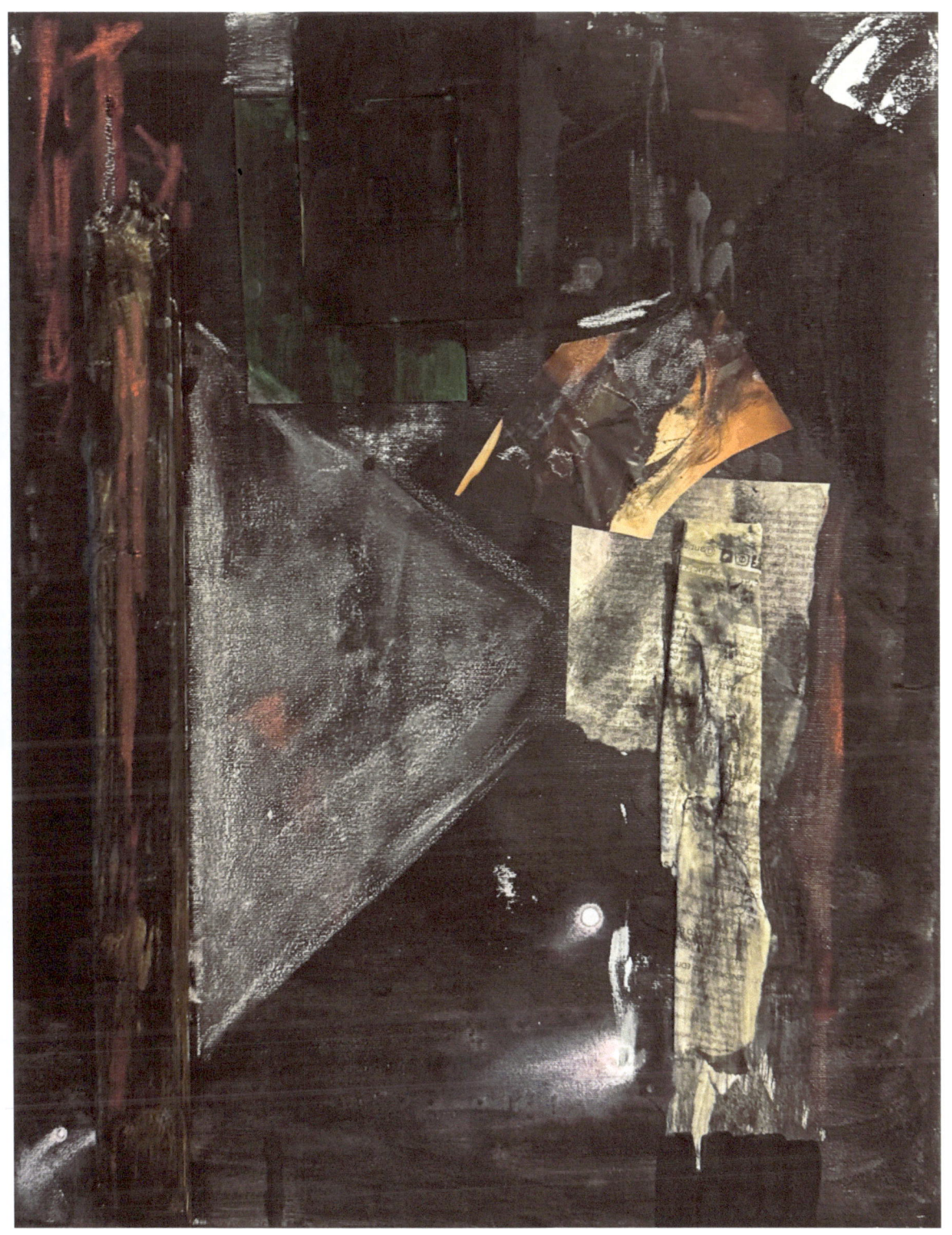

*Trash* (mixed media, oil, ink, glue, collage on canvas), Max Flanigan

BUZZ KOZAK

# Zero Food Waste

Sometimes when I am force fed my NyQuil
I am thrust back to Frost Valley, my arms
carrying my body through the sycamores,
hand in adolescent hand, peeking through the
blindfold, the "exercise of trust." It's the one time
I see color in my eyelids, and it's the one time
my palms are not sweat creased enough where
I need to apologize.

                    I slouch in the passenger seat, mechanical—
                    it's all cursive. Upstate rumbles hit the flatbed,
                    then the flatbed folds in.

Christmas light panopticon above our
tethered bodies, a boy asks if me and Will
are dating. I say "ew," as one does, but
my face sort of flushes and he notices this.
We go to eat dinner (chicken fingers, of course)
as the sherbet sky fills the cabin walls fecund,
and I wonder if it really seeped in
that much—unabashedly, doors open—in the moment.

                    We hit the driveway backing in. My dad doesn't swear,
                    a whistle will do. I offer condolences, a shoulder pat, but
                    my arm doesn't move.

We curdle in the courtyard to walk a hike,
I think, and we're at the age where the boys' hands
cast a bigger shadow when they raise them, brushing
flannel-topped sweaters, catching leaves in the hoods, and
I eye Jack's for hours wishing my shoulders were
*that* broad, my arms *that* quarterback, healthy red freckled arms.
The ground is still offset and the sycamores taunt me, offer
leaves at my foot.

                        The door opens the door and my flower stem hands
                        break the windows, whoops! And the slog into bed warms me up
                        until                I cough again.

BUZZ KOZAK

# 40mg Omeprazole, Once Daily

he left me
        corroded, rust bucket
gut,

diseased:
we're all falsetto now.
                it's the black plague!

i know F major now,
        ammunition too heavy
to carry.

he's sprawled across bedsheets,
windows,
        two blankets, so

leg untouched
                leg,
twitching eight counts in REM.

oil spill molars,
bile-lubed joints,
                wound

open on the mantle. on the
Tiffany lamp.
              half-soldered scraps

turn to mirrors.
        check my form in the
cracks,

warped and mangled, phrase
               lost
in translation,

in arms and metal and contract    and release out
my                                         mouth.

BUZZ KOZAK

# Reservoir

volcanic eruption.
i'm throating canoes.
again i eye the door like sport.
again i crease the edges
of *GRE Test Prep*,
furrowed and damp.
sweat blankets scribbles.
i've given up reason,
bubbling "C." let's think
        diagonally
                now.
let's think every fit boy
who orders a latte
is dolled-up Bushwick
Mormon, pinstripe jeans
to the ground, knockoff
Uggs tracking in dirt
& chipmunk laughter.
           it seeps into decaf.

the reservoir's hazy &
              furtive,
all brown and polluted,
spilled onto our muck-kissed asses.
it's tremolo and it's booming,
but i can't    find the note        anymore.
is the mud still caught in

your soles? or has the snow
washed it over?

the Starbucks door
kind of vibrates
when it opens, and
my skull        bursts        dandelions,
bellows amphetamine rush,
a head fuzz reaction,
quake-shiver-tummy-ache.
spaghetti blondes
                peek
from the corner. perched on
royal shoulders, kind-hearted
shoulders. a
                rotation &
his stance is alien,
not quite fag-handed
enough to be catalyst.
hound-hunkered,
blue collar voice drumming low.
okay, there's no boats. okay,
hose the damage.

vesuvius calms.
i bubble "C."

BUZZ KOZAK

# My 4th Annual Birthday Political Fundraiser

i sleep a sleep gone fifty. "help wanted,"
the corner-bound cardboard coaxes mosquitoes,

eats the lilies alive, rotisserie-style, charred, up
for barter with some other vulture. auction off

my sociability, arranging plates, utensils. steak knives.
i'm eager to serve a grand masquerade, proof of life.

i'm an earnest jew, i think, generosity and such.
a few interns, the hill, knights of the round table,

my pride. dead hydrangeas—-a classless landscape, but
no pity, no "woe is me," me. some freak accident

turned me mute, yes. sorry for no letters. sorry
for the late checks, the long hours. for the cause!

the keyed fold-out table is wrinkled with age and
the fruit collapses on it in a gust. i gainsay

this succumbing, the seeds on the ground,
but my square glasses turn round in the sheen.

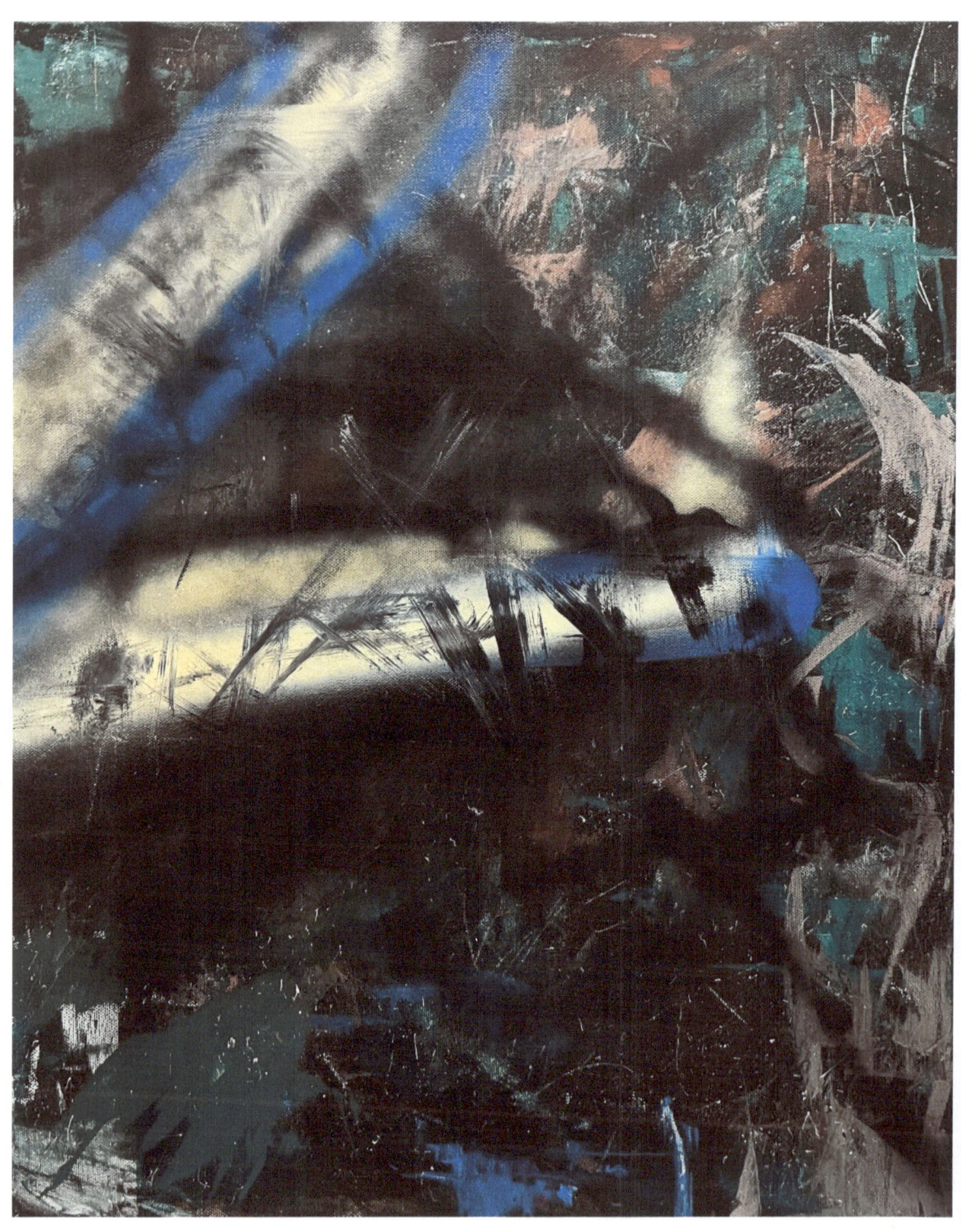

*Riptide* (acrylic and ink on canvas), Sawyer Taylor Ramsamooj

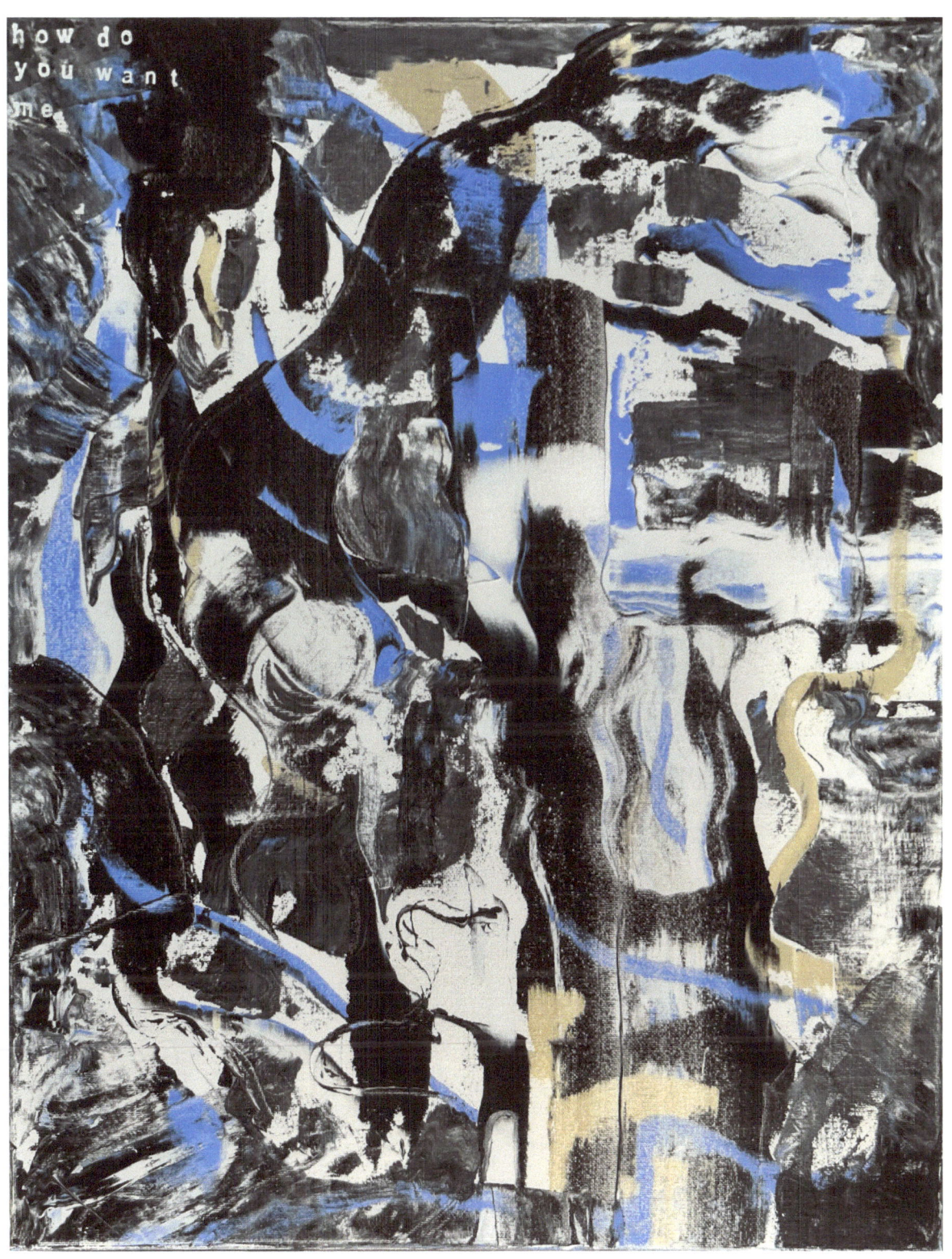

*how do you want me?* (acrylic and ink on canvas), Sawyer Taylor Ramsamooj

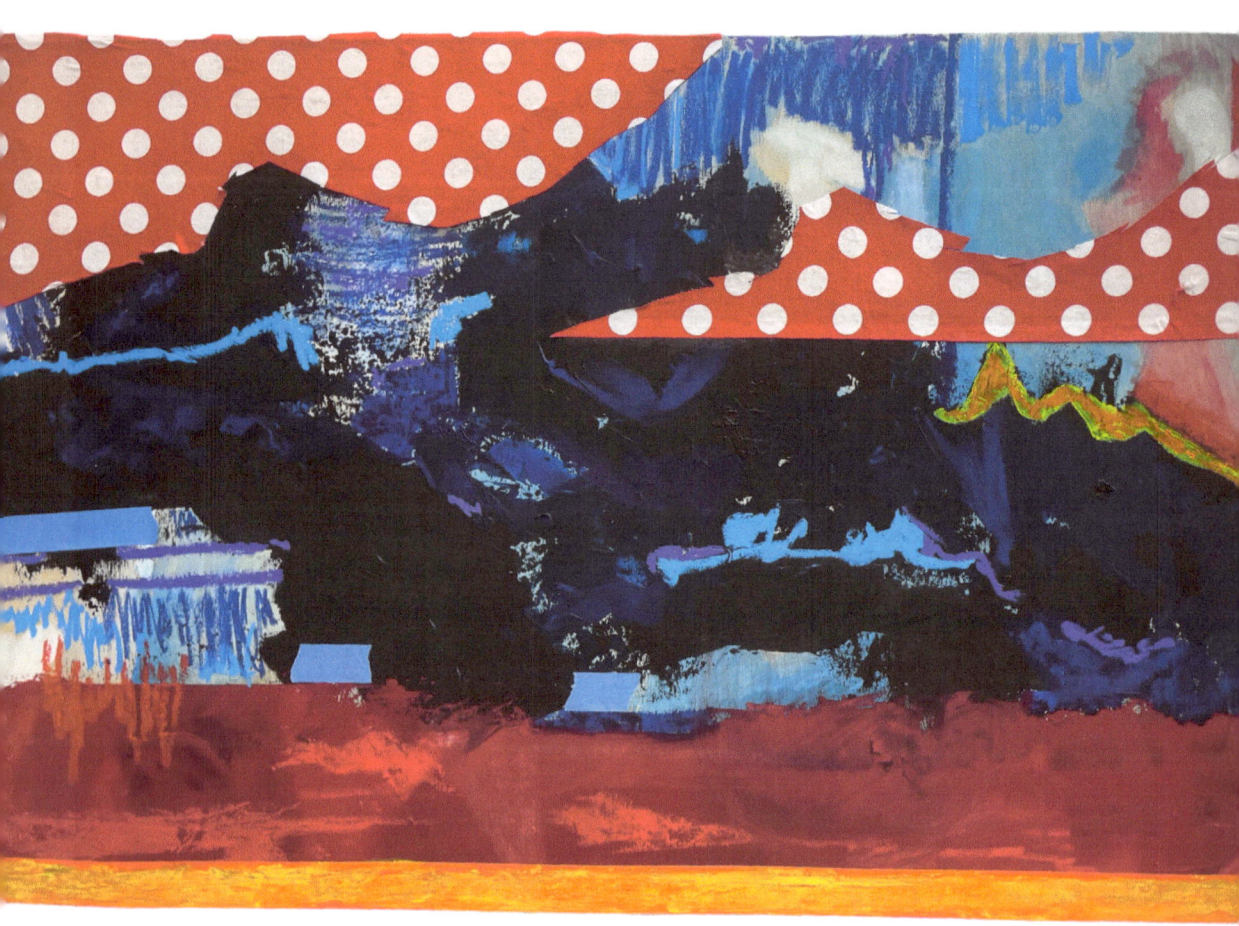

*Horizon* (mixed media, oil, ink, fabric, crayon, tape, on board), Max Flanigan

SAM CARRILLO

# Madrid

I fell asleep last night to the echoes of Madrid
Cheers of "¡Vale! ¡Vale!"
Of decade old friends who have eased their way into old age
As a tired body slides into a warm bath

In their accents, I can picture their eyes crinkled with years of laughter
Like candy wrappers left in a pant pocket
I can see their tanned skin polka-dotted with freckles, ripened by the sun
Plush with the richness of jamón serrano and the sweetness of sangria
I feel the kiss of the soft evening air
Brush against my cheeks
As their linen pants sway with the breeze
They are not dancing, but it's close enough to flamenco for me

In the narrow streets I hear echoes from corners I may never reach
Walking between rust colored terracotta-roofed buildings as they make their wedding vows with shadows on the cobblestone streets
I am walking and I see cigarette smoke reaching up towards wet laundry hung out to dry in the summer heat
The sweet smell of burnt herbs and tobacco pairs well with a beer and some tapas, or so I've heard
I didn't know Madrid would have me writing poetry
It's hardly poetry—

Just some things I saw as I fell asleep

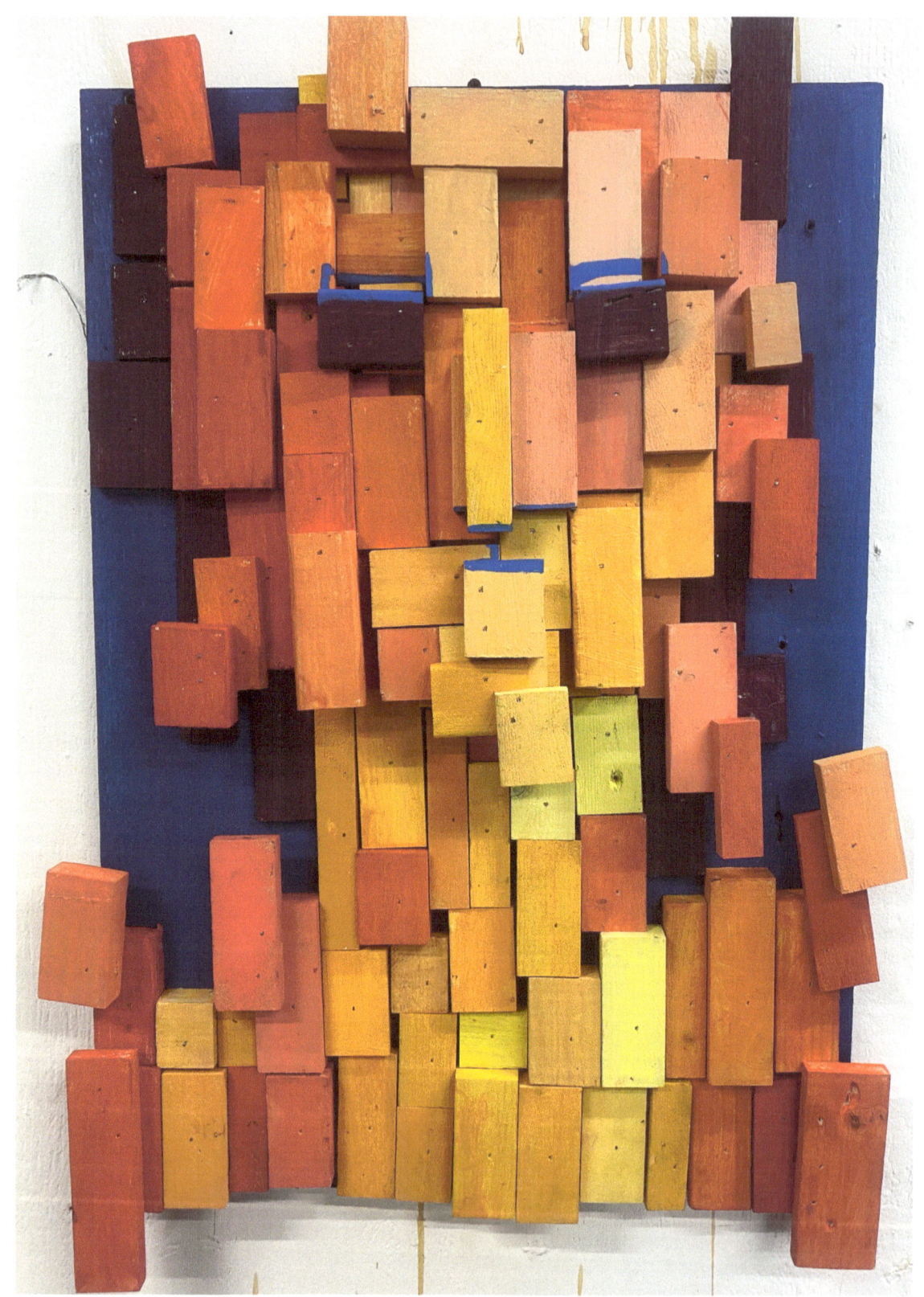

*Self-Portrait* (acrylic paint and wood), Natalie Vazquez-Martinez

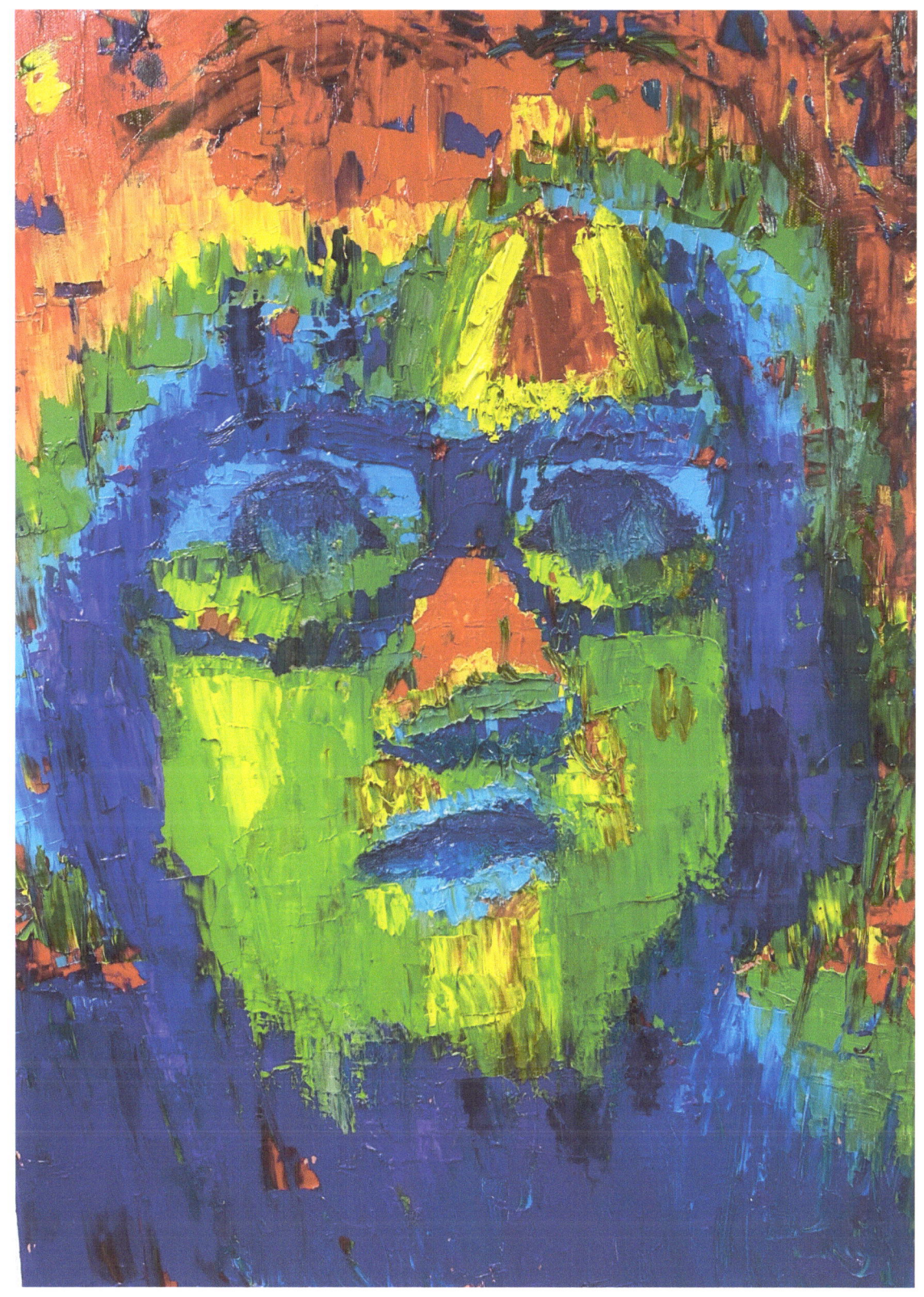

*Me* (oil on canvas), Natalie Vazquez-Martinez

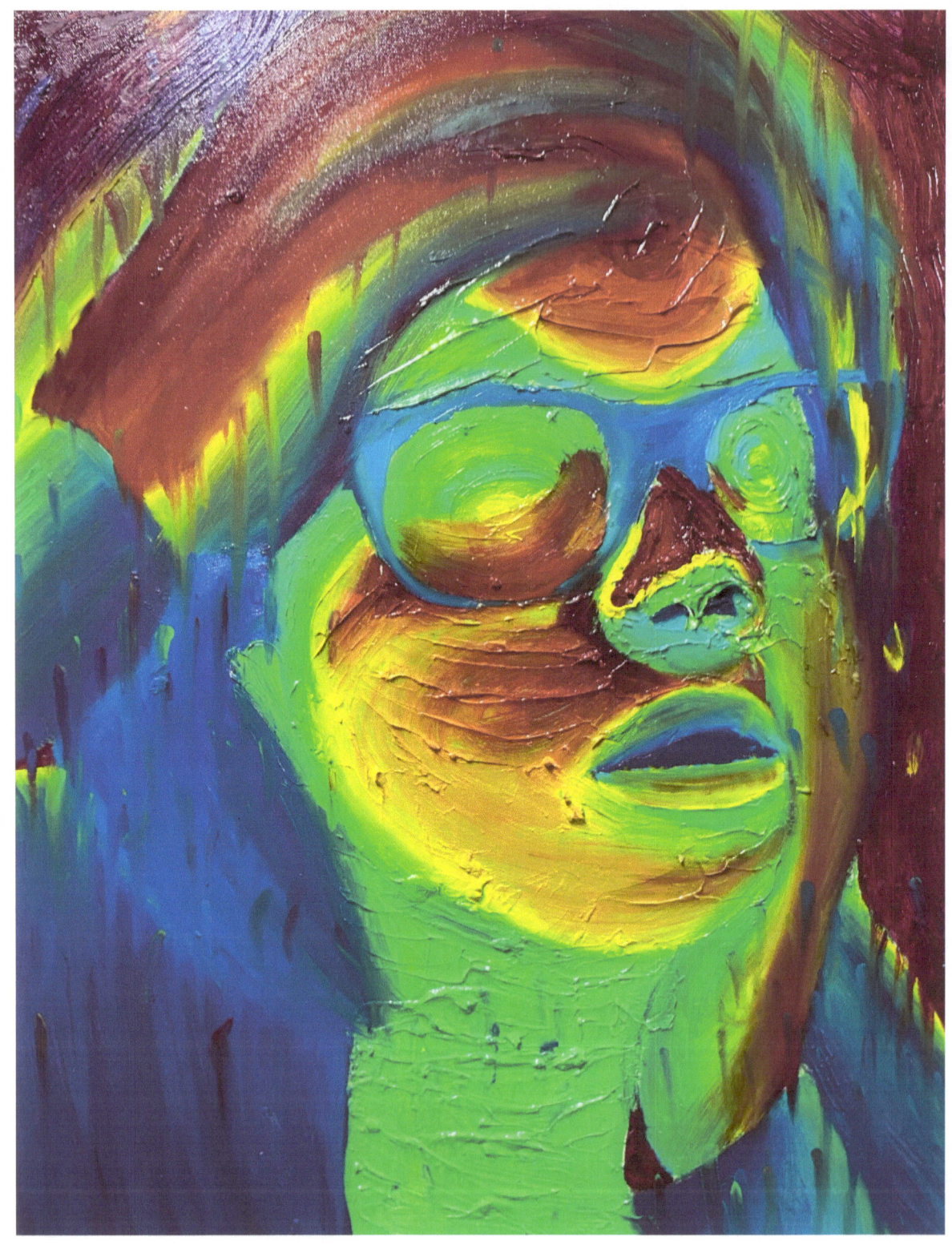

*Moi* (oil on canvas), Natalie Vazquez-Martinez

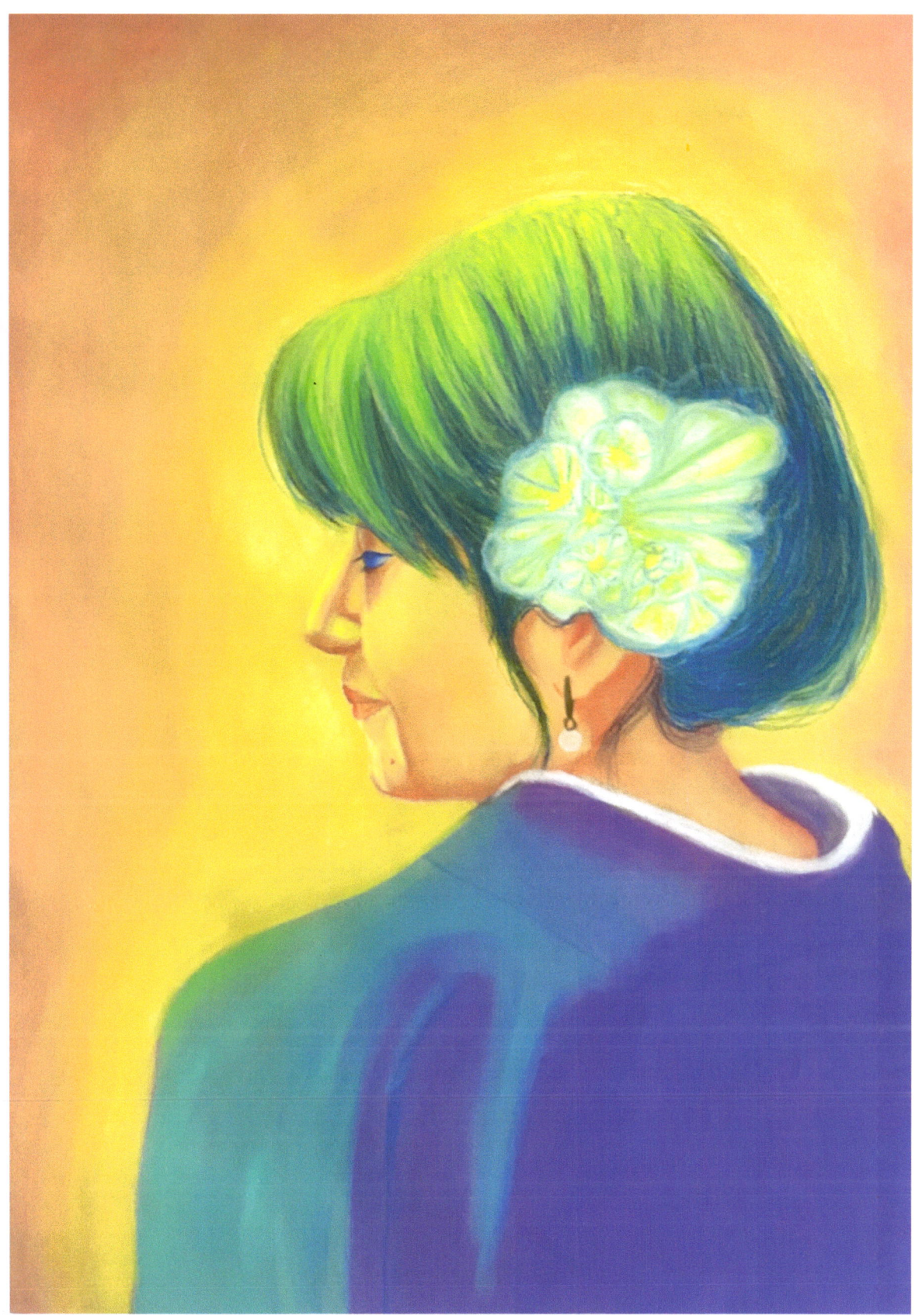

*Leslie* (soft pastels and colored pencils), Natalie Vazquez-Martinez

REY DAVIS

# In the Face of Nothing Else

If you can be nothing else,
be kind.

Even if you are forgotten,
and the wild falls apart,
suppose that the flowers will think of you while they wilt;
the bees will carry your sweet song in the pollen;
and the wind will whistle your tune when it rains.

While cruel rapids thunderously shake the tender earth,
let your kindness be wellspring to the flowers.

Never forget,
that you too,
are the sun that rests on the patterned deer's back.

Never forget,
that I too,
will think of you fondly
while the wildflowers whisper their gossips through tendrils of truth.

Because,
in the face of nothing else,
you stayed kind.

FICTION

KATERINA RONCONI

# Fingertipped in Wait

She has the sauce pot on a low, low flame; the extra virgin olive oil, a thin layer just glazing the bottom of the brown burnt pot, expires before it sizzles. That perfume, the smell of expiring olives, compels her to slit the garlic clove with her sharpest blade.

He sits over in the dining room, at the head of her table; she's all over the stove for him. She's making him her pasta-and-sauce. She's spent days grating her parmesan cheese to top it off, preparing it with all the bits and pieces of her love for him. The glass jar brims underneath the lid with all the soft yellowed shavings.

She'd made this pasta-and-sauce before for her other loves. The last time had been for Dave. Dave didn't get it. He had piled himself on top of her like lumps of sugar in black coffee—it only coated the bitter taste, slippery and poignant. He had left her with that taste. And he said she'd chased him away, right after eating her pasta-and-sauce.

That hurt. She'd just shared herself with him, and he had spat it out, her DNA, right there onto the table. It was the nail clipping that had done it for him.

That's why this time she'd make sure not one nail shard got into her pasta-and-sauce. Because that had stung. That nail clipping Dave spat out caught right in her eye, so that even now she can feel that itch every time she blinks.

She grips the rim of the sauce pot and tilts it so the oil spills into a pool in its curve. She drops in the garlic. The runny oil catches it fervently, spurting ecstatically; the clove bathes in its embrace. If it could sink anymore into it, it would.

The garlic sizzling, the olive oil sizzling, their breaths marry into one delicious, long, shuddering exhale.

The heat condenses around her face, budding right on the button of her frigid nose. The olive oil squirts against her cheeks in fast-fading stings. She pets them into her face, tsking. She's let things heat up too much. She can't let it burn and spoil her extra virgin olive oil.

Like Dave did. He just pulled up in her, in her driveway, house, and bed last year. He had pulled in all too fast and cleaned it all out. He left not one hair in the drain, on the pillowcases, in between couch cushions, not one lick of dead skin, not one flake of dandruff; he had gone bald while he was with her. Because of his fast-falling hair and splintering scalp, he got sick in the head and shaved it all off. If only he had grasped her at all, he'd have seen that she loved him, hair shedding and all. She ate it up.

Dave left her with nothing left behind at all. Except that bitter, slick taste like the thick-smelling garlic pushing up in her nostrils right now, not that she'd let things heat up too much.

Cringing, she takes the pot off the burner, setting it on the metal corner of the sink. How could she have ever called him a love? Forking out the gold-branded garlic, she tosses the used- up clove into the garbage bag hanging limply from the lower cabinet door.

Her sights shift over to him, her love. He's waiting for her, his gaze gnawing at her. Her lips quirk, spreading. He's gnawing his nails like his eyes gnaw—and will gnaw—her whole body.

I'd let you eat me up, she's whispering under her breath. I swear, Love, but not yet. Wait there patiently; this pasta-and-sauce is only a condiment to what this all really means. Trust, Love, trust.

She pours the carton of tomato purée into the pot. The oil hisses, spitting as the tomato purée cools it out. Easing the pot back on the burner, she stirs the two fruity excretions together.

He catches a whiff. He smirks. He gets it.

They got it together the other week in the car. The windows wept all around them. She nibbled at the dead skin on his lips, got it right between her front teeth, peeled, and swallowed. Now, he always wears his lips chapped for her because she loves him that way. The way he wears them chapped—licking them dry at the table, even now—signaled to her that he really got how she loved, especially how she loved him.

Since the first time she laid her eyes on him the other month, she had a strong sense he'd get it. His lip was between his teeth when their gazes met. That's when she gathered how much he truly understood the value of his skin. That's why he chewed his lips and nails; he kept it all inside of him, storing it up to finally release to her, in her, when they'd get it together in the car, in bed, in the kitchen, and, soon, at the table.

She plucks the lid from the drying rack and leaves it half open over the sauce so the oil and tomato can ruminate. Then, taking the pasta pot from the rack, she fills it three-quarters with tap water and puts it on the highest flame beside the sauce.

Leaning back on the counter, she watches for the water to boil, but her eyes keep flickering over onto him, her love. Each time their eyes meet she fights the urge to get more of a taste of them—to get her tongue tip right between the grooves in those deep brown, rippling irises.

But, of course, she couldn't do that. She didn't want to bleed them dry, she didn't crave the iron-tinted aftertaste of fresh-left blood at all; Dave had taught her that. His lips had always been too soft so that when her teeth caught on them, they broke his skin and he'd bleed.

Skin feels, not blood. Skin carries what her love feels; her touch on him and his touch on her. It's all in the skin. All the fingertips that had grazed her and gripped her and held her—they were all over her skin, all up in her pores, saturated in her skin-lines and fingerprints, all the touches of her past loves that had left. Especially Dave's.

She shudders. The thought of that touch arrests her body in a spasm. She whips out the once wedge, now rind of parmesan cheese from the deep pocket of her apron along with a plate and cheese grater from the cabinet. She must channel these feelings into love-making.

She scrapes the cheese against the grater, grazing up and down slowly, slowly, gently letting her fingerprints get caught here and there with the rind. They sprinkle down alongside the parmesan onto the plate. She's thinking of him, her love, of their love—oh, how she loves him—of love, loving, and how all her other loves didn't get it like he does.

She breathes: you're different, Love. You're more than just my head; you're my body. The others couldn't grasp this, but I knew I could make you; not just this, but all of it, all of me; not just my skin—my crevices and curves, like they grasped, dug deeply into when we joined really only a few inches deep—but my flesh underneath, my swollen, gamey heat and soul.

The salt of the parmesan stings the bits of rawness across her fingertips. She lets the rind fall beside the grater and sweeps all of herself from the plate into the jar. She brushes back her hair, some strands clinging to the rawness, desperate to be included; she wraps them around her fingers and snaps them into pieces, sprinkling them into the parmesan.

Her dad would be disgusted; he always insisted on freshly grated parmesan for pasta-and-sauce. But this is her pasta-and-sauce, almost ready for her love.

The timer rings and she drains the pasta, sliding it into a bowl and pouring the bright red sauce all over it. She opens the jar, finally, and holds her breath as she peppers it like snow in small heaps all over the pasta.

She sifts for nail clippings as the yellowed flakes soak into the sauce. Did some slip in? Some nails?

But what if her love didn't like her hair? Would he spit her out like Dave did? But no, she distinctly recalled that one time, when he cooked pasta and vodka sauce, she could see one of her hairs caught with the spaghetti on his fork. Didn't he look at his fork, noticing the strand swaying loosely, and then smile and eat it?

Wasn't that one of the signals that cued her into knowing that he got it?

She hugs the bowl of pasta tightly against her stomach, letting it warm her entrails and heart as she sweeps out of the kitchen. Her skirt licks up her calves like white-hot flames, fizzling against her hips as she plops the bowl of pasta down on the table.

Love, he says, it looks delicious.

Doesn't it? She scoops the whole top layer, with all the parmesan, onto his plate. It'll taste even better, dear.

She sits at the other end of the table, plate in front of her for the sake of decorum. Their eyes meet as he takes the first bite. He chews slowly, pressing his tongue against the roof of his mouth and letting the sauce suffuse over it; the pasta bits part for the taste of the parmesan to leech through.

His eyes close. There's not much flavor, he notes. The cheese, I mean.

The memory of the nail clipping stings her eyes. She blinks a small smile at her love. She lifts herself from the table, slips into the kitchen, and grabs the jar. She bites the inner part of her lip, tastes the bitter blood, tastes all her loves who left her. With a stiff gait, she sets down the jar in front of the plate. It's still halfway full.

She won't impose on him. She won't pile herself on top of him. He'll have to take her as he pleases.

Sitting back down, she watches her love take bite after bite. After bite, after bite.

Her insides burn all the way down; the corner of her lip twinges, watching him consume it all. But will he really accept the hair, the nails, the skin? Will he take her, served up on that plate?

Her heart is bursting from anticipation, from the blood of her past loves, from watching her love. His hand—it reaches out for the jar, stuffing inside, squeezing a handful in between his fingers and palm.

He pulls out, releasing the shavings onto the remaining penne.

Warmth spills over her legs. With haste he eats, forkful at a time, fast yet steady, right to the rhythm of her memories, of the bitter tastes of her loves, of her twisty DNA: in, out, in and out.

He gets it.

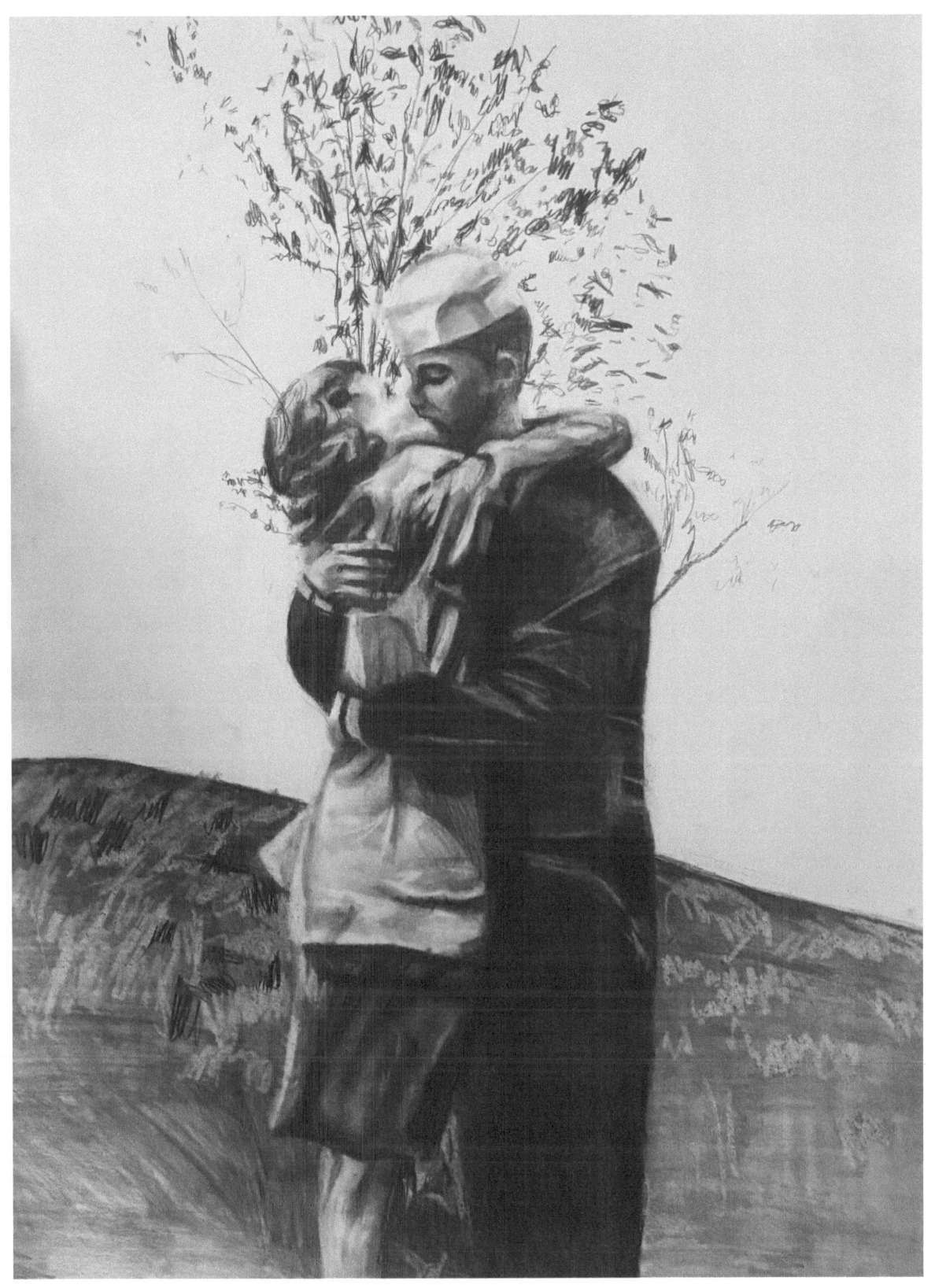

*Bring Him Home* (graphite and charcoal on paper), Michaela Chittenden

BELLE ELYSE

# malpractice

my boyfriend smelled like bandaids,
injected insulin, medicinal cologne
his bedroom door would close
with doctor's appointment formality
both naked in hospital gowns
raking over me with surgeon's eyes
dropping my daily diagnoses
he urged treatment urged hospital
my armchair doctor not unloving
and when my inpatient ended
and i checked myself out
and walked myself home
he hung wanted posters boasting
how he knew what was wrong with me

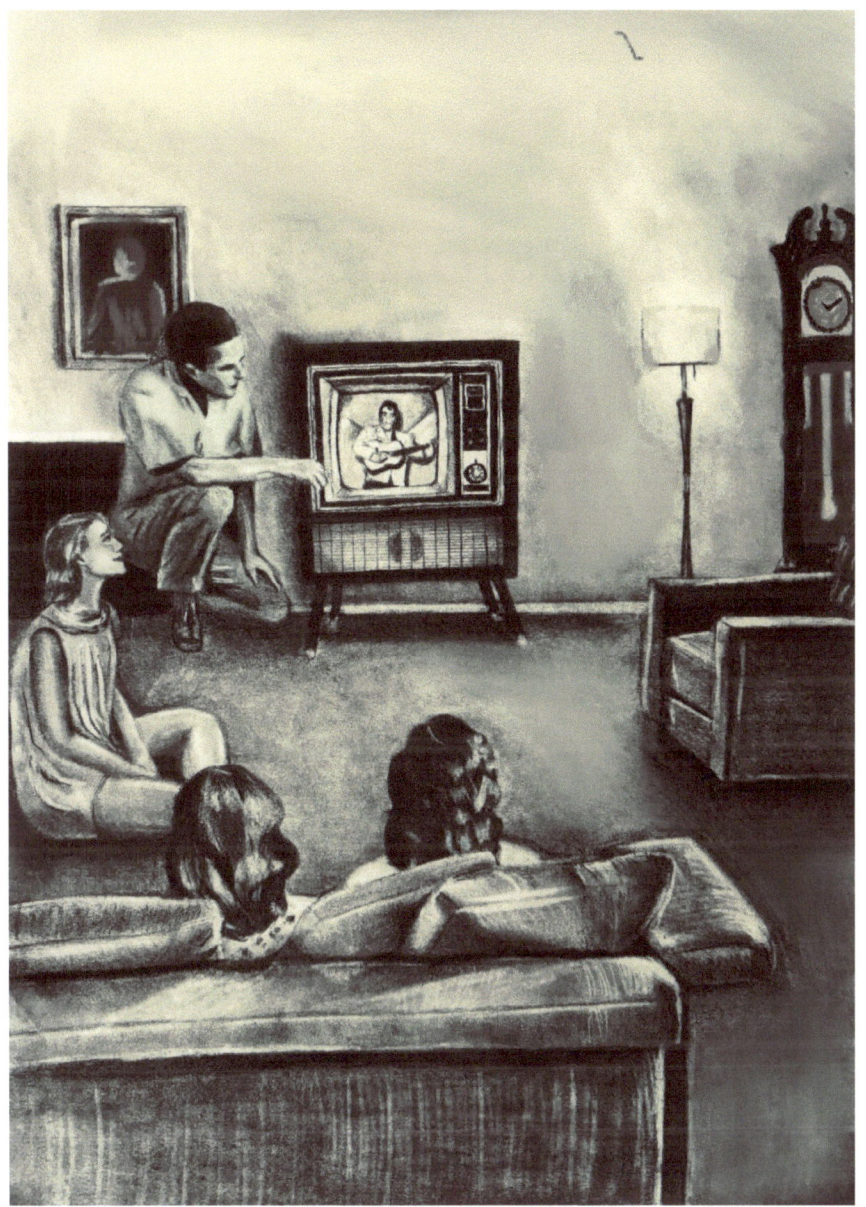

*The American Dream* (graphite and charcoal on paper), Michaela Chittenden

STEPHEN PIAZZA

FICTION

# Confessions

It was a suicide, of course, and though I think the Church has changed its position on the matter in recent years, his extended family retained older sensibilities, and the casket was closed to avoid the cousins from Pennsylvania asking too many questions. I saw his Aunty Lyra, and his cousin Andy, who married a divorced woman and adopted her daughter. That's why they moved; no one liked that.

His kin were important, and he had wanted me to know them. That was one of his things, when we were all sitting on chairs with itchy, red upholstery, four years ago at the Campus TransMasculine+ Support Circle. That was the first time I met him.

"Hi, I'm Thomas, and uh, three fun facts about me: I'm the youngest of seven, and I went to Catholic school, and I like cats."

In the process of trying to avoid looking at the group leader—a junior with hair dyed blue and green—his dark eyes had landed directly on me. Seven was my lucky number. It was auspicious.

Reaffirming my memory at the funeral, I realized I retained more information than I supposed I had, though I had always wondered what his family knew of me. The winter after the support circle, upon finding out we lived a mere hour away from one another, I visited his house, a charming little Tudor with a white front door, met four out of six siblings, and ate leftover panettone and salmon from Christmas. They were friendly, overly friendly, in the way Italians are, but Thom, strangely, became colder to me. Always avoiding touch until we were alone in his little room, his hands, trembling, excited, would dance at the ends of my hair, my shoulders, and upper arms. Kissing me once on each cheek, he was shy and bold at the same time.

"Should I have come as a girl instead?" I thought I passed well enough at that point that they wouldn't know.

"No, no, you're fine, they know how I am. They just want me to dress nice for the holidays," he said as he slid off his pinafore and came even closer to me, hands dancing.

After the funeral, I was put in charge of room cleaning duty, which, though arduous and unpleasant—which is why they shunted it to me—was surprising. I was a nobody. I told Bethany, his eldest and favorite sister, as such and she said, as if it couldn't be more clear, "You were the best friend."

His ex-friend. More than a friend. Thom had never called me his boyfriend; not to my face, at least. It was only *my friend*, or, when he was at his best, his happiest, *my dear, my Ollie*. Mostly just *you*. But semantics didn't matter, and I found myself back in the little room. It was sort of green-gray, though in the February light, it just looked gray. It had belonged to one of his elder brothers and then he and Barbara, another sister, had shared it, and when Barbara had gone to live in Syracuse after undergrad, it was his to keep.

The mother couldn't talk to me—well, she couldn't talk to anyone—so Beth had explained the job. She sounded all right, but clipped, clinical, far away.

"Everything we're going to keep is mostly out of here. Anything with a yellow Post-it should go down to the living room. That stuff's going to go out to Pennsylvania; they've got more storage there. Whatever's left goes into bags, and that'll go down to the garage—we'll just throw it out." A pause, and then, a little softer, closer: "Oliver, you're welcome to keep anything." I shrugged, and she left me to it.

It took longer than it should have to get everything downstairs for the Pennsylvanians: a bookshelf still full of Young Adult fiction and poetry and a Marilynne Robinson work I had given him for some birthday or Christmas; his bedside lamp, taken off the top of a table that I was told would stay in the room; toys he had shed since childhood but remained hidden in the closet and under the bed while he went off to college. Some little things—whatever his family had not seen as meaningful or relevant enough to keep but too specific for the Pennsylvanians—remained. Thom's Saint Sebastian portrait was still hanging up, destined for the bag. That was a gift from me too, albeit a smarmy one.

Our first date, though neither of us called it that, was at the Starbucks across the street from the University—a choice made in spite, since I worked at the Dunkin and loathed it.

"Catholic school, huh?" I said over an oat milk latte. "That sounds dreadful."

"Oh yes," he replied, twisting the knotted friendship bracelet on his wrist around and around. "They made me wear a uniform. A girl's uniform." When he got excited, his pretty cow eyes always went a little wider, a bit buggy.

"Hm, did they force you to go to Church too?" I had no idea what Catholic Mass was like, being born to slackful Presbyterians and deliberately atheist myself, but from what I knew of it, it was droll. All that sitting and standing and kneeling.

"I liked going to Mass. I go to the 10 a.m. a block away from here every other Sunday."

"…Oh."

"Is that bad?"

"Nothing, I—I'm just surprised. With you being…"

"The Church is very good about trans people!" And Thomas, with a flourish, began to prattle on about something having to do with Pope Francis, who I thought was the Polish one, but in fact was not, and under the table, beneath all the layers and boots, our feet were touching.

Our first split happened after I had met his family. His cow eyes were glossy and red when we saw each other again in January.

"I don't think this relationship is working out," he said.

"Is it your parents? Was I disrespectful? Are you all right?" I touched his shoulder, and he flinched.

"No, no, you're fine, I just can't—with a guy—" And he started crying again, and I did not, testosterone having burnt all the tears out of me. We did not speak for a week.

Then, he came to my dorm, wanting to talk. He'd said about five words, teasing me for my unmade bed when our knees touched and he leapt on top of me, kissing and biting and clawing at my shirt like he was trying to tear beneath it and rend my flesh.

I loved sex, and loved having it, though, typical for our kind, most of what I had with Thom consisted of us rolling about on the bed and rubbing up on one another until one or both of us came (or neither of us did, and we simply tired of the sweat and the spit). Thom wanted it, surely. His eyes always shone a certain way, his hands, greedily, heavily, running up and down my waist and legs and chest—but right afterwards, he'd always get up, leave me cold, go into the bathroom, and wash or cry or do something else I was not privy to.

I had already gotten dressed by the time Thom was back, grumbling something about cravings and intrinsic disorders.

"So being trans is fine by you, but being gay isn't?"

"Well—yes!" He went on to say, well, it isn't about being gay or desire; it's about action and choices.

I wanted to hear very little of it, until he said, in the middle of his spiel: "I mean, it's not like we can have children!" He always spoke a little shrill.

"…So you and a cis man?"

"Let's not talk about that," he said, and patted me on the head, like one would a dog, or a child.

Rolling up the portrait to go into the trash, I felt my cheeks twitch, filling with heat and melting into a frown. I had no right to be angry. I was not Beth, who had been the first to hold him, after his mother. I was not her either. I was not Barbara, who swapped scary stories with him from the top bunk, or any of the unlucky six. I was not the friends or acquaintances from college or church, who'd find out through a third-party text. I was not the one who had to deal with his financials, or the funeral arrangements. I was not the one who found him.

Thom and I had not even been friends at the end—something of my own doing. And yet, my fingers were still tearing the paper corners of the print, angry at Thom for leaving me to clean up his mess, to throw out the things I had bought him, for killing himself and binding us forever when I had wanted to leave, for choosing to die rather than be someone like me.

We remained chaste for most of our friendship. The longest (and final) interlude we had gone without, ah, *knowing* one another had lasted for more than a year. When it would happen, it would usually come with tears and another break, though we could never stay away from one another long. We were both psychology majors (though he was on the education-psych path, and I planned on going into law), and loved to read (though I preferred memoir, and he fiction), and took our tea with lemon and our coffee without sugar, and, outside of that support circle, had very little taste for getting to know the rest of the transmasculine student body, who were too theatre kid for me and too hedonistic for Thom.

I did have needs, and on occasion, they'd be satisfied. I tried to be discreet about it, because irrationally, though he'd never call it a relationship, I'd feel a little of the guilt Thom must have felt constantly. Once, he told me he'd seen me walking alongside another man that weekend.

"And is anything wrong with that?"

"You do what you want," he said, smiling, but his nostrils flared, and I knew he was angry.

One of the books bound for Pennsylvania had escaped my notice: a copy of Augustine's *Confessions*. I knew what was written inside: **PROPERTY OF TH. C. RIELLO**, and throughout the margins of the book, little scribbles and underlines. *So beautiful. Must remember this. Show O.* He'd carried it around constantly sophomore year, until the corners of the pages went round and smooth.

I knew that his opposition to my sexual proclivities was not just possessiveness (though, in my petty way, I hoped it was), but an attempt to save my soul. Thom never said anything about it; he wouldn't dare. Even at his most zealous, he was never fire-and-brimstone, but in his way, I could tell he wanted to evangelize to me.

"I wish I could do the things other people could do," he told me once, late at night, while we had taken ten minutes off from studying for finals to sip Keurig coffee and chat. In my dorm, I wore very little, and Thom was watching me stretch my bare legs, eyes shining. The last time we had slept together was four months before, which led to Thomas ghosting me for three weeks.

"You only live once," I said.

"No," he spat bitterly, "we don't, and that's why I—can't. Isn't it so sad to see it your way? That this—this is it?"

Well, I suppose his way was rosier, but for all I knew, his laugh and his tinny voice and his hands and eyes were gone to me regardless of whatever lasted into the next life, covered in six feet of overturned earth. I would take the book with me, one of only a couple things I'd take. There were some notes in my pocket too, mostly schoolwork, that the family would not want to keep but were ephemera of his I could not bear to know were thrown away.

To Thom's credit, he was no hypocrite; he spent as much time sorting juice from milk donations at the Interfaith Food Pantry as he did preaching to me, and in that sort of Christian activity, I joined him happily.

One of the best memories—one of the last, only weeks ago, when we were both happy—came after some holiday supply run I had done with him. The afternoon light was strong by the time we finished, and in Thom's little room, the green-gray had turned a bright, pale sort of color, like springtime. He laughed happily, a tinkling of silver bells, and he had held my hand and brought it up near his mouth, and I thought he would kiss it, but he merely blew some air on it. His breath was warm.

It was late now, and the room was dark and sparse. Almost everything was out, and when I moved, I heard the empty echo of my shoes on the hardwood floor. The bed and the table that was beside it were the only things that'd stay. They put anything they'd found on him, in his pockets, after, in the table's drawer. Well, the family had the note; I hadn't read it, but I knew that I was mentioned. That's how they knew to invite me to the service. Whether he cursed me or apologized or said goodbye, I didn't want to know.

The last time I had been in the room, before now, and after that warm, buttery day, was a week or so afterwards when he had called me over for—for —I couldn't remember. I couldn't remember. I shook a little, and I had to grip the bedside table so my legs would not fail me.

Whatever it was I was there for, I was there, and sitting on Thom's bed, and he was next to me, our sides close enough that I could feel the heat radiating from his body, its absorption into mine. He always ran so warm. Was he cold when they found him? Or still warm, so close to life if not for the silence where his heart should beat loud, clear, strong enough that I could hear it, however far away?

I had laughed at some stupid joke he'd made and thumped Thom on his back, and we looked at one another. It had been a year for me, and a little more than that for him. I stopped laughing, and his eyes shone, and he said, sweet and shrill as ever, "Oh, *Ollie!*" nd then we were kissing, and again, and I was laughing.

He had whispered to me, during, "I love you, I love you, I love you more than anything, I love you more than *everything*," and I sang out, cried aloud, echoed him.

After, I shut my eyes, hid my face in between Thom's chest and his inner arm, serenaded by his healthy, living heartbeat, my own arm clutching whatever it could hold of him, hoping that if I slept, he would not disturb me and break the quiet, serendipitous moment. *This,* I thought, *is my Mass.* But too little time had gone by before he was up again, out of the room, and my eyes stayed shut, hoping he'd come back and hold me. After some time, I got up too, and went where I'd never gone.

He was vomiting. We had barely eaten that night, and it had already come up, but Thom was still heaving dryly into the toilet, his back rippling with violent shudders.

"I-I shouldn't have done that—" Another heave.

"Was I really that bad?" I had tried to be clever, breezy, but it came out much too raw and made me sound wounded.

"I wasn't supposed to do that. I wish I hadn't—I shouldn't have done any of that—I'm sorry, I'm so sorry."

Thom had told me time and time again that it was just about sex, carnal desire; love had nothing to do with it. *No one loves love more than God*—but what he had said to me was fresh in my mind, its sweetness going sour, and I knew when he apologized for everything he was apologizing for that, too.

"I'm going to Hell," he muttered. "It's over, I'm going to Hell."

I was suddenly sick of it, all of it, the years I had spent feeling dead, and virginal, and judged by him, waiting for the moment he'd decide he wanted me, the way he'd cry, and guilt me and leave me, and I'd be lost until he decided he didn't hate himself anymore and would come back, rinse and repeat.

"And what about me? I'm the same as you; I'm worse, I'm an *atheist*, where am I going?"

Pugnacious, I did not know what I was challenging him to say. *Oh, Oliver, of course you'd be saved. I would never believe in a God that would damn you!* Of course he would not say this, but there was still a wild, romantic, puerile part of me that wished he would. I was dirty, still shirtless, sweat and cum cooling between my legs, and the more he muttered, the filthier I felt. I wanted him to kiss me, clean me, and though he would not, I still did not expect Thom to go slack-jawed, turn from me, back down to the toilet, and say, so quiet I barely caught it:

"I…I don't know…"

And that was it. When I got home that night, before stumbling into the shower, drunk off a case of Stella Artois, I texted him: *I don't think this relationship is working out*, and turned off the ringer.

The last time we spoke, I was retrieving the jacket I had left at his place, a $150 winter coat from Zara, though I'd had it for so long the pockets were starting to felt up and some buttons had been lost to the wind. I didn't want to stay long, so I left the car running to give me some excuse to zip off as soon as I could. He produced the coat quickly, but as I turned to go, he reached for my hand and murmured, "My Ollie…"

"I'm not your anything," I said.

Then I was gone, and then he was gone.

I didn't let him have it. But, remembering this, I pressed my hands together, and though mine were bigger and rougher from years of the hot water and carcinogenic dishwashing liquid at Dunkin, I pretended one of them was Thom's, and that my touch had damned him, and saved him, and he was here now, packing up his things, not to go into a moth-infested attic in Pennsylvania or some trash yard even further than that, but perhaps to a cramped little flat we had bought together and were thinking of moving a cat into.

The moon shone in through the tulle curtain—it was due to snow in the night—and I wanted to leave Thom's family well alone. After this, I would have nothing more to do with them, and I was sure they did not want me here now that the work was done. But before I did, some curiosity took hold of me, and I went to the bedside table.

I opened the drawer. I closed it.

Eyes blurring, I crawled into his bed, sheets neat and square, and I wondered if it was Thom's doing, before he did it, or his mother's afterwards. I put my face to the right pillow, the one he liked to sleep on, and I sniffed and sniffed for a whiff of him, but I couldn't smell anything. I cried knowing that my tears were washing away whatever was left of him: his eyelashes or skin cells or sweat, which only made me cry harder.

"Tommy, Tommy, Tommy, I'm sorry, I'm sorry," I said, though I didn't know for what, or for whom. To Thom, to me, to God, who I had never wanted more to be real. "I'm sorry, I'm sorry."

In the drawer, there were two things: a wrinkly, dustless little Bible, and buttons from my coat.

PAULINA BARGNESI

# The Misfortunate Family's Limerick

There once was a dad who lived in a basement
The mother had made the arrangement
Both couldn't take the screaming
They were better off leaving
But they took their marriage as their only achievement

There once was a son with the blues
Who would chug down all this booze
The counselor told him it ain't right
But he'd still do it throughout the night
And that's why his screws came loose

There once was a daughter who stewed in her silence
She was tired of her tyrants
Her bags were already made
There would be no barricade
She would leave their violence

**OWEN PENHOLLOW**

# My Method to Slightly Mitigate the Harm of Wealth Inequality

It really pisses me off
When I see a building that's named after
Some great former president of the institution,
Or a Civil Rights leader,
Or a ground-breaking scientist,
Instead of the most heinous rich person you can imagine.

Hear me out.
Think about how cheap your dorm would be
If it was called Bill Cosby Hall.

Let's take advantage of the guilt of the wealthy.
If Pharma Bro wants to repair his image,
Let him pay to name a hospital;
Everyone will call it some asinine nickname anyway.
I don't know who the fuck these buildings are named after in the first place,
But I know healthcare is expensive.

In short, I wouldn't take my kids to Epstein Island,
But I'd take them to the Epstein Elephant Sanctuary
(If it was five bucks cheaper).

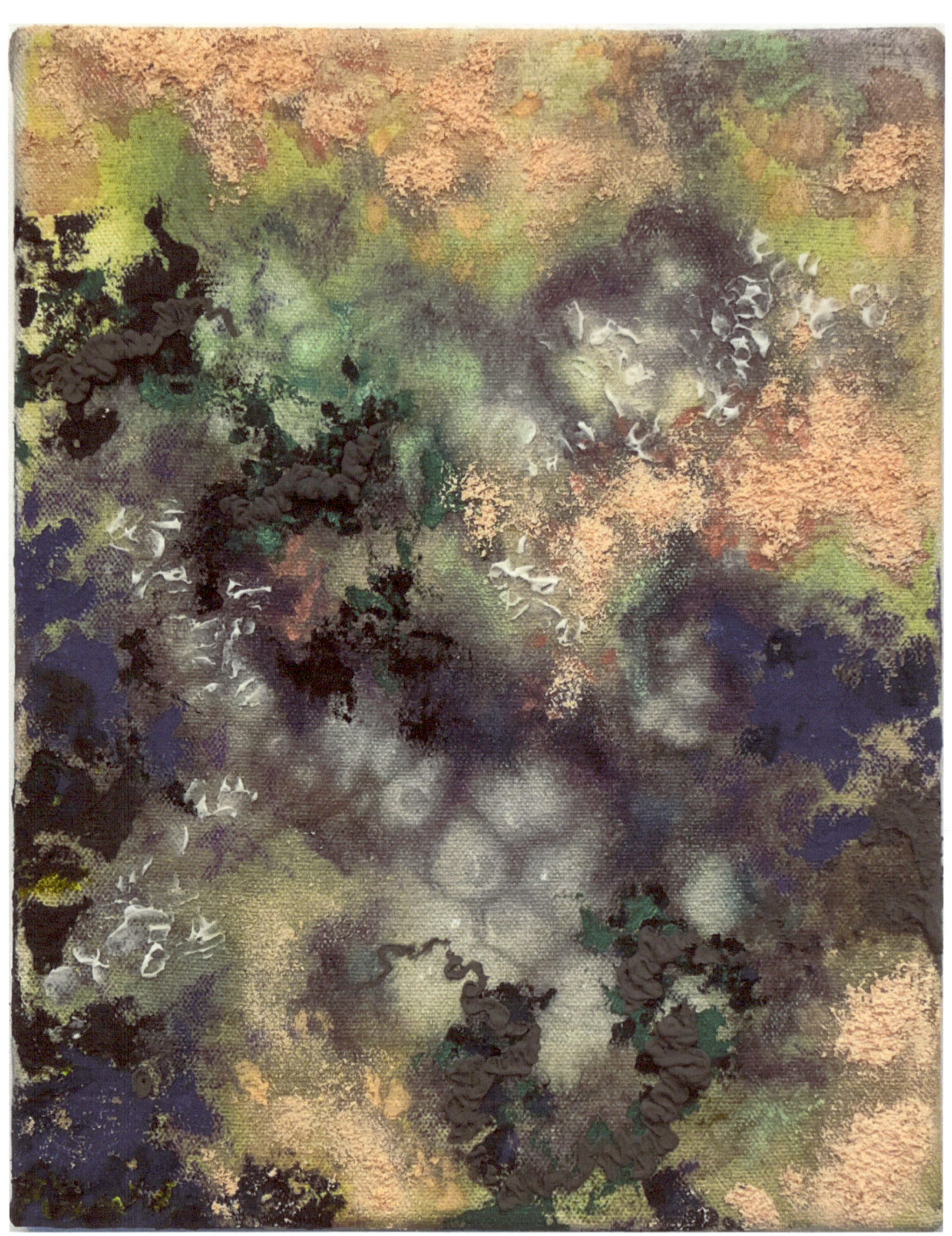

*Mold Study* (acrylic, modeling paste, and watercolor on canvas), Victoria Stiver

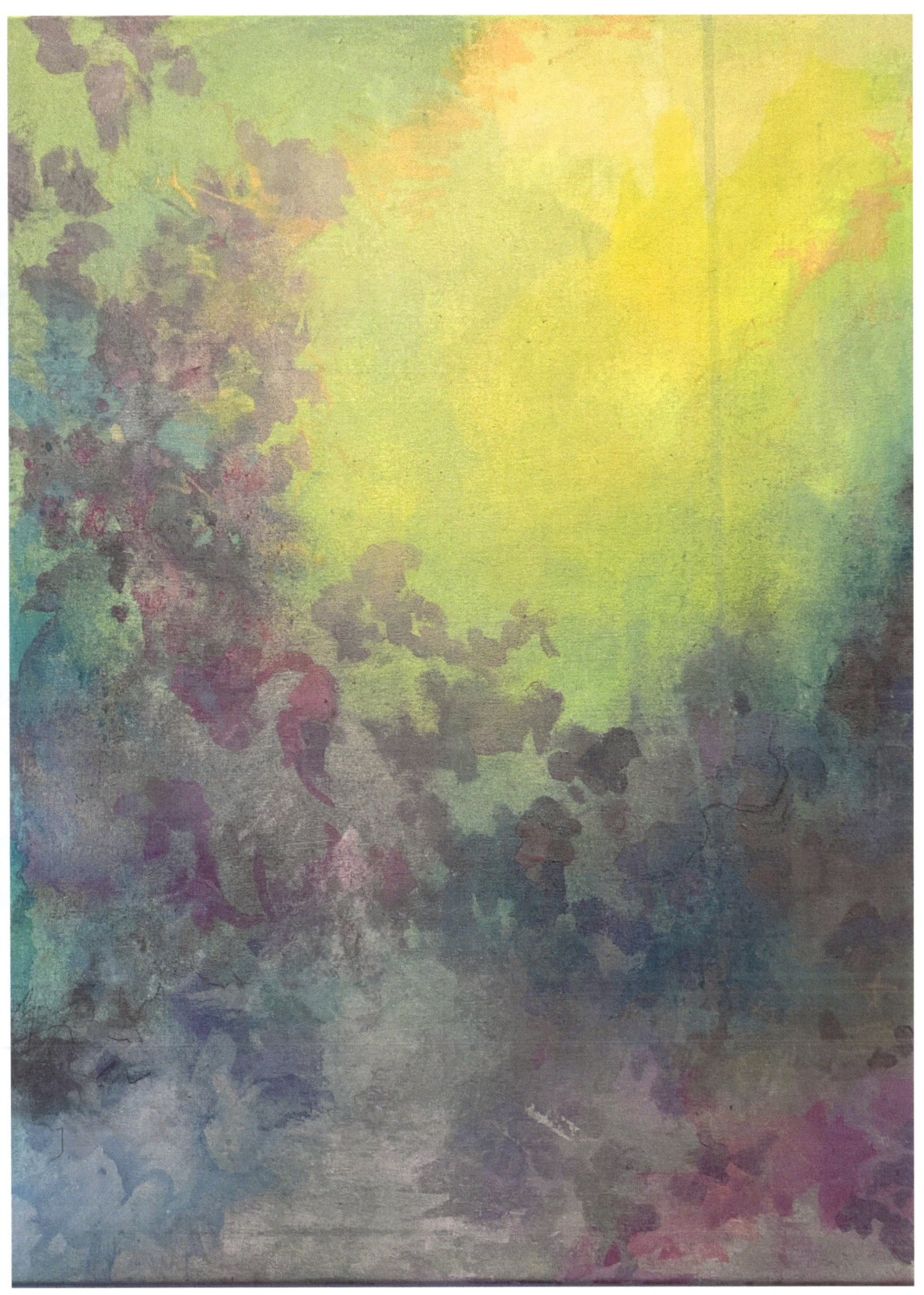

*I Know It Exists Because I Feel It With You* (acrylic and graphite on canvas), Victoria Stiver

ANA PAUL

# Lemonpoem

Lemon tree, lemongrass
Sunday Morning, Sunday Mass
The terrain I traced between the lakes
A great barrier
Great love
A grave mistake
Take my hand, take my wisdom
Take me lonely, take me fully
Take me dancing, take me now
Procure a wedding, write a vow
Lemon hair, lemon face
Crystal eyes, a diamond gate
Will you take me? Will I escape?
Take me here, take me there
Write me letters, braid my hair
In a jiffy, in a rhyme
You hold my face, give you my pride
Lemon tree, lemon flower
I dream upon the emerald tower
Like a river, like a lover
Like a lucky counted clover
Flow and turn and take me gently
Slipped right past the heartfelt sentry
Lemon tears, lemoncholy
Sting and churn my lemonpain
With a blade that cuts the vein

Citrus lover, citrus mistress,
Cheating babe dipped in hibiscus
Undercover, undergarment
A laugh turned out to be too charming
But in the end, it's lemonlaughter
A citrus fruit for ever after
Lemon joy, lemon jolly,
Reverting back to lemonfolly.

ANA PAUL

# Lovers' Moon

I bathe myself in lovers' moon so that gardenia flowers will grow out of my temples
And lovers will circle my nipples
As if that will make more white roses sprout from my chest
You'll remember me when you're in the garden
With other flowers and perfumes
And an idea catches your nose and invites you over
You'll remember me when you turn corners to see who's selling melodies wrapped in
Painted cardboard
You'll smell lovers' moon and think back twenty years
Thinking we should've gone to the backseat so that we could speak and sleep and maybe whisper the daily news to each other
As you caress my thigh with your gentle violence
And you smile
So wild
At my indulgence
Kiss me
And bury your ancestry in my neck where the flower still blooms
Inviting nobody but you

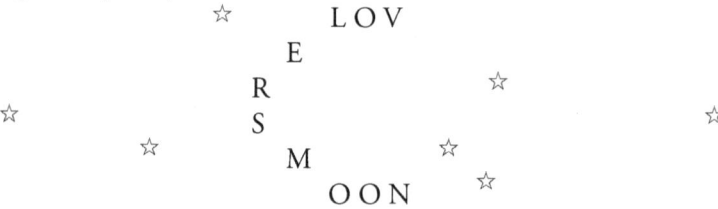

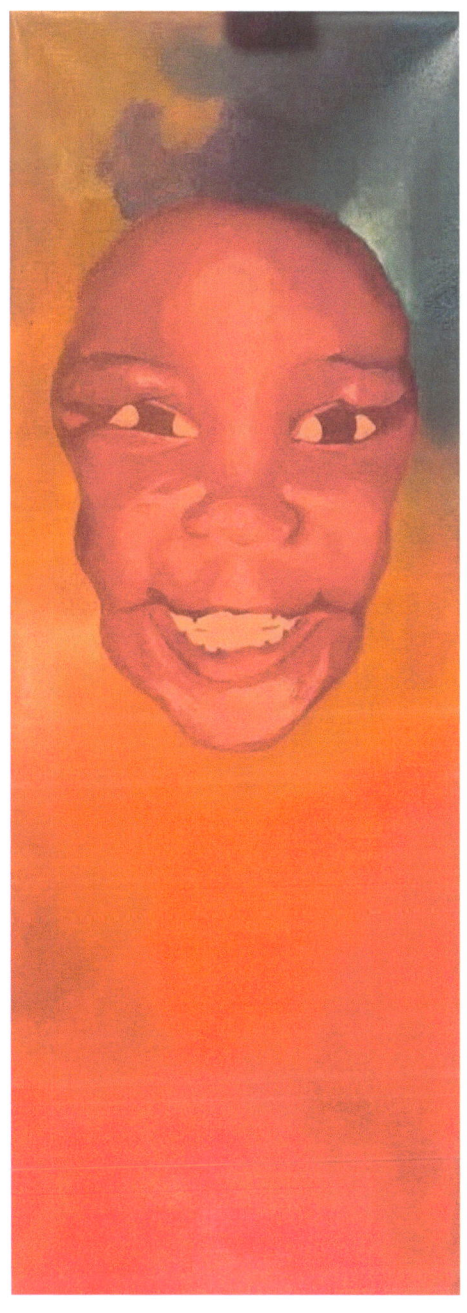

*Maliboo (Little Brother),* Shadae Walker

MICHAEL CROWLEY

# Subtropic

**"Yes, New York City is now considered to have a humid subtropical climate"**
reads my Google searches' AI overview.

*When did that happen?*
*Oh wait it's been?*

The *New York Times* says the same.
goodbye maples, birches too.
The figs are out the burlap,
Jesus, we can't go back.

An old pear watching over
three pawpaws in my yard,
grow well in Eden's climate
planted last spring, to time it.

July & August's usual joys:
fresh Champagne mangoes
hit the stores, our pears ripen
and Dad's juicer overflows.

But September's awfully warm out
Boulder rolling leads no where
I pace myself gainst' burnout
'gainst temperate warfare.

I guess I'll picture mango trees
right by my pawpaws and my pears.
some I think I'll plant, in threes maybe,
and pray the good lord beware,
and hope they're taken from me.

MICHEAL CROWLEY

# Beach Day

Withered oaks bar cracked gray
from black sands, silent witnesses
of a Great evil, done by us.
Memory of a people, corrodes, rusts.

Molted & melted shells
freckle our morbid lane,
acid rain & sea foam mix
burn away our claim.

Boiled fish flock to this beach.
New currents unknown
swept those poor souls
to strands, lands, not home.

Dark mangy birds pick the eyes
of a pike washed up,
fly to their nest &
to their young, they'll sup.

The last of us,
fierce hunger fueled,
crawls from the mossy gray,
through the leafless oaks
stands on black sand
& covers their nose
& digs in.

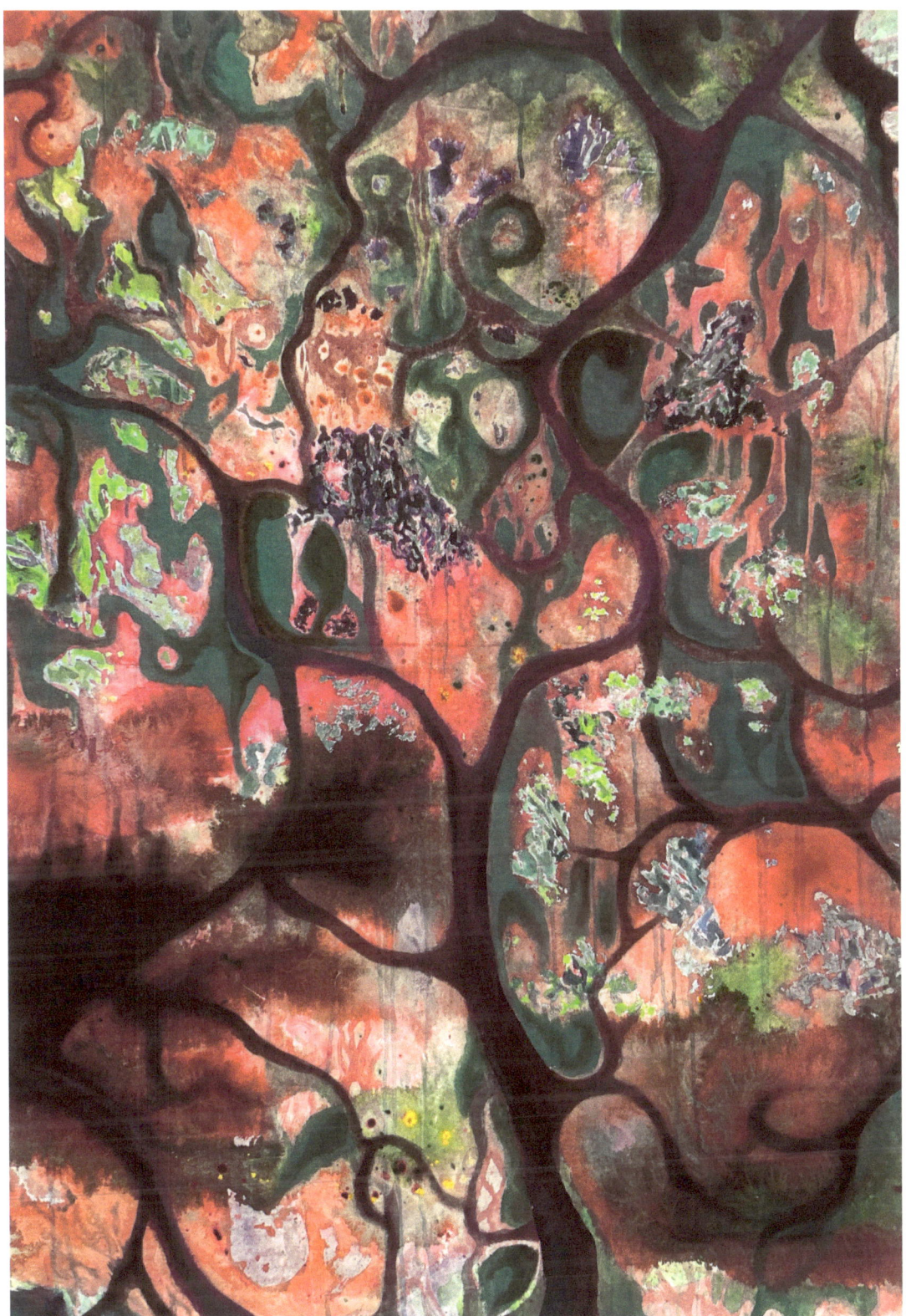
*Heartland* (acrylic on canvas), Emma Eager

LORI YAMOND

CREATIVE NONFICTION

# The Womb Shaped Fruit

The pollination process for a fig does not start with an alluringly structured flower or a vibrant color, but rather, it starts with a smell—sweet and enticing, drifting through the air until it tickles the senses of a female fig wasp, who is zipping around some feet away. This smell will attract her to come closer to the premature fruit with a promised whisper that sounds of the word *safety*. But the female fig wasp does not follow this smell laced in safety for herself. Instead, she seeks it out for her children, wanting them coddled and cradled in a valley of tiny flowers hidden within the temptress fig—flowers whose petals act like bassinets for growing and rowdy babies. And so, to get to this safe little nursery, the mother wasp must torture herself. She must squeeze through the narrow opening at the bottom of the calling fig and endure the tight space, sacrificing her wings which are ripped off her back, while ignoring her antennae as they get pulled out from her delicate face. Once inside, bruised and battered, the female fig wasp will visit as many tiny flowers as she can. She will give these flowers the pollen they desperately crave, but she will also drop her children inside of them—a goodnight kiss farewell and then down into the bassinets they go. This wasp will die, deep inside the fig, surrounded by her unborn children. She will be satisfied by their safety because this is her life's work, her one and only mission—to be a mother, and to live and die solely for her offspring's prosperity.

 The male children of this late female fig wasp will hatch first, knowing nothing of her motherly drive and feminine devotion. Her male children will be fixated on only one thing: impregnating their unborn sisters with belligerent motivation. Like the fate that should be bestowed upon all violating men, these male children will tunnel their way out of the fig and die with no memorial, no life, no importance. The female children, now pregnant and left behind, will make their way out of the tunnels crafted by their rapist brothers and fly out into the sunlit world, ready to repeat the same labor as their mother.

Before even truly maturing into the fragrant and juicy fruit that we love, the fig will be labeled as an executioner, a womb, and a coffin.

My mom used to drive a black Nissan 240SX before she was married and had kids. The 240SX—a sports car made for professional women in the late eighties and early nineties—was her everything. It was the greatest companion to her job as an accounts receivable, which she got after being the first daughter in her family to go to college—a degree she paid for all on her own—and the car matched her leather pumps, black briefcase, and fur jacket perfectly. My mom met my dad when she had this car, and it was a piece of their whirlwind romance, like the packet of green apple gum they traded back and forth between offices and cubicles with love notes attached.

When my mom got pregnant in 1997, she sold her black Nissan 240SX because she couldn't fit a car seat in the back. Every time she tells a story about this sports car, it always ends with a mournful sigh and a proclamation that she misses the car deeply, but she had to put being a mother and the safety of her soon-to-be son first. My mom gave up her car, and the next thing she knew, she was giving up her job, and after that, she was giving up her apartment for a house on Timber Road.

A few months ago, my mom was talking to me and said, "I don't like my life." She said that she missed her job, missed wearing her leather pumps, missed having a black briefcase to carry around, and missed shrugging on her fur jacket in the morning. She said that she missed driving her 240SX.

In January 1963, Sylvia Plath published her novel *The Bell Jar* in the United Kingdom under the pen name Victoria Lucas. The beloved work wouldn't be published under her own name until 1966—and even later. In 1971, It would finally be published in America after years of upheld family wishes over the sensitive autobiographical content found within its pages. For many readers, one page has always stuck out in particular—a page found in chapter seven which meddles in the metaphorical property of the fig tree.

For Esther Greenwood, the novel's main character, the fig tree stands as the image of her life, reflecting back to her directly and beckoning with dozens of possibilities. She describes every possibility as being a plump and teeth-rotting fig—so sweet, so full of life, the red center like a beating heart pumping blood into the body of happiness. To one fig, Esther attributes being a famous poet, to another being a successful professor, and to another being a mother: a happy mother, with happy children, and a happy husband. But like all fruit, figs do not stand the test of time, and before Esther can satiate her growing hunger for a sweet life, the figs begin to rot on their branches and fall to her feet.

   Esther walks away hungry, never getting to taste a good life, with black fig flesh sticking to the soles of her shoes.

After tucking her two children into bed on February 11, 1963, Sylvia Plath committed suicide through the inhalation of carbon monoxide by sticking her head into a gas oven. She died deep inside her London apartment, one room over from her sleeping son and daughter, doors closed and towels sealing up the gaps where wood met floor, ensuring their safety.

Human beings often attribute the feeling of warmth with love and security. We are created in the warmth of bedsheets, we grow in the warmth of wombs, we love the way sun-warmed grass feels under our bare feet, and the way a warm mug feels between our palms. Is our love for warmth an excuse for the greenhouse we have locked Mother Nature inside of? She is pounding at the glass with fists made of wildfires, and kicking at the metal structure with feet as strong as glaciers collapsing into still, arctic waters. She is watching her children gas the land and life she has built for them, and she is watching as they call it survival, listening as they call it thriving.

   Mother Nature visibly mourns the beauty that has been destroyed at the hands of her human children, destroyed by her act of being a mother who gives it all up for her small ones, who gives them everything as they take, take, and take.

Eighty million years ago, somewhere in West Asia, a group of primates—who would eventually evolve into the complex human beings we are today—were picking figs off trees for consumption. I imagine these creatures lying out on their bellies, under the warm sun, savoring the fruit one bite at a time, or using a finger to spoon some of its mushy flesh into the mouths of their children. They must have enjoyed the fruit all year round, for figs thrive in warm conditions—tiny spheres of life, not particularly fond of the cold.

   Yet the humble fig is a fruit that endures, meaning today, gardeners all around the world grow and harvest them, even in places that face harsh winter months. The key to such endurance is survival through dormancy, especially for fig trees living solitary lives in large pots. When the first winter chill drifts through the dry air, fig tree owners are urged to expose their trees to it, letting the cold take hold, and haul the fruit bearer off into a deep, dormant slumber. The trees should then be stored in a cool, dark place until the time for growth comes around, once again.

I was hauled off into a winter of dormancy when I witnessed my mother cry in front of me, openly, for the first time in my life. Her tears were the first exposure of icy winds that blew and commanded my soul into a space of cool, grief-stricken darkness that would last for the rest of winter. I remember these moments of exposure so well, yet I don't remember all the time I spent dormant. But then again, isn't that the whole point? Dormancy is a survival strategy, a way in which living things can endure the coldest of periods, the bleakest of days, and the harshest of feelings.

It started in the haze of sleep and the pounding of wind and rain upon the glass of my window, in the room I used to share with my sister. The woman in me now, who studies literature, can't help but look back on that awful rainstorm and note the perfect symbolism to reflect the ruin about to come. It was around three in the morning on Christmas day, when my mother unexpectedly came into our room and sat down on the edge of my sister's bed, directly across from me. I awoke in a fog to my mother saying, "Girls, girls wake up." And I knew from the fragility of her voice that she was crying and when I gazed up at her from my pillow, I could confirm this from the makeup—which she shamelessly sleeps in—that was rubbed off her face and streaky with fresh, salty tears. In the mixture of Christmas excitement, sleepy confusion, and noisy rain, my mother told us that our grandfather had passed away only an hour earlier. A day celebrated for holy birth now curdled into an endless stretch of years marked by death.

Although my grandfather's death would come to disturb me later—with horrible memories of his funeral and tears of grief mixed with shower water—what disturbed me most in the moment of hearing this news was my mother crying. I had never seen her cry before and I was puzzled by these tears she shed over her father, because most of my life had been defined by her disliking her father, who wasn't just the man she called "dad," but also her abuser.

I realized that night—the night which conjured up my very own winter of dormancy—that our love for people can also become dormant. The physical abuse that my mother experienced at the hands of her father, pushed her love for him into a dormant space, dark and cool, only to be broken open when death came knocking and announced that the love no longer needed to survive, because it no longer had a place to go.

When I enjoyed a cracker with leftover cheese from our Christmas charcuterie platter that year and slathered a helping of Dalmatia fig jam on top, I could barely register the sweetness—could barely get the image of my mother crying, out from behind my eyes.

I think the difficult task of coming face to face with your mother's fragility has caused human beings to turn their backs on the land that has nursed them through it all. We wish to turn a blind eye to the pain ravaging the woman whose motherhood has labeled her as resilient. Maybe this blind eye has given us the courage to be the ones to cause the ravaging pain…

Demeter wandered Greece in hopes of finding her daughter, Persephone, alive and safe. Persephone, who was cherishing the beauty of a spring meadow, picking flowers among nymphs, was suddenly torn out of youthful peace and abducted by Hades, getting hauled off into the Underworld without a trace.
 Her mother, goddess of Earth, goddess of harvest, giver of fertility, plunged the world into barren despair with tears of wicked pain dropping to the green landscape, turning it brown and cold. She searched for her daughter far and wide, being let into the homes of many Greeks. One home was tended by the king of Attica, noble Phytalus. Phytalus could not give Demeter her daughter back, for he was no Orpheus or Odysseus—men wily enough to descend into Hades' realm, with only prayers to return them above ground safely, once again—but Phytalus could give something else, and that was kindness to this hurting mother; this king was a giver of grand hospitality.
 To show her appreciation to Phytalus' warm embrace, Demeter gifted him a fig tree, which would bear sacred fruit that would be honored by many people.
 In the end, Phytalus harvested a fig, and Demeter walked away, still with no daughter.

Scientists believe that hundreds of thousands of wildlife species have gone extinct at the hands of human beings. Do you think Mother Nature is wandering her land in the hopes of finding them alive and safe?

When I was eight years old, I had a really bad accident on the playground during recess. A few kids playing tag ran into my back, causing my face to smash into a pole that was holding up the bars of the jungle gym. It happened so fast that I didn't even register that I was hurt, not until I looked down and saw blood dripping all over my purple shirt, down onto the wood chips that were softening the hard earth. Another student nearby must have seen the gore and my tears bursting, because she quickly ran to me, looped an arm around my back, took hold of my hand, and led me off to the nurse's office. Stuck in my brain is this awful image of my crimson blood lining the hallway floor in tiny droplets, a map from the main entrance to the baby blue nurse's quarters.

After the nurse assessed the damage and placed an ice pack on my battered face, my teacher showed up and informed me that my mother had been called about the situation, and that she was driving over right away. I needed my mother so badly. I needed her comfort and her soothing words, but all I could think about was her seeing my blood lining the hallway floor, and walking into the nurse's office, overwhelmed with horror at the sight of her child hurt.

A lot of people I know are woefully aware that my biggest fear is blood, and I think this accident is the origin of that queasy fear. Yet in a lot of ways, I think I fear blood because it means that this body, for which my mother gave up her whole life, has been damaged. It means that I have given my mother another image of her child in pain to keep her up at night worrying.

Mother Nature is on her knees begging her human children to stop hurting the Earth, for she cannot watch their bodies and homes endure any more damage at the hands of these harmful inflictions. The images of her children choking on smoke, dropping dead in extreme heat or seizing up in extreme cold, of their belongings getting consumed by floods, and of infectious diseases taking hold, each one a new worry line added to her skin; each is a new cross Mother Nature is forced to bear.

My father is sitting in our family den nursing his crippling anxiety and depression with a bottle of Xanax and a package of Nabisco Fig Newtons, while the green Genoa figs in his garden go from ripe to rotten, dead before their owner can muster up the courage to go outside and harvest them.

My mother is on the couch next to me, whispering while pointing in the direction of the den: "When is it my turn to hurt? When is it my turn to be in pain and lie down?"

I fight the urge to look at her and whisper, *Mommy, don't you know that you traded in your life of comfort for a family? Don't you know that in this unfair world, mothers do not get to rest.*

When we feminize the land and call it our mother, are we saying that it is perfectly acceptable to hurt a woman? In our feminization, have we accepted the fact that our land is weak and fragile and overly emotional, that she can probably handle all of the ruin raining down on top of her, with no rest, even if she acts dramatic about it?

We call the land our mother because we need her. We drink her water like milk from the breasts, and we lay down on her solid ground like babies in need of skin to skin. Yet we have forced the land to be our housewife, in charge of raising ungrateful children, in charge of pleasing the family, even as she yawns with exhaustion.

Within a life marked by motherhood—a life devoted to the safety and prosperity of her kin—the female fig wasp only finds a moment of rest amid the act of dying.

I cannot let my mother, or our land, be the female fig wasp.

## Works Cited

Cordova, Justin C. and Young, James B. "Lady Lazarus: An Insight into the Suicidality of Sylvia Plath." *Methodist DeBakey Cardiovascular Journal*, https://journal.houstonmethodist.org/articles/10.14797/mdcvj.1481.

Higgins, Susan. "Pollinating Figs: the Inside Story — Fig Wasps." *Lewis Ginter Botanical Garden*, https://www.lewisginter.org/fig-wasps/.

North, Allison. "10 Fascinating Facts about Figs." *Roots Plants*, https://www.rootsplants.co.uk/blogs/features/10-fascinating-facts-about-figs.

Plath, Sylvia. *The Bell Jar*. London, William Heinemann Limited, 1963.

Scott, Ian. "Sylvia Plath's "The Bell Jar" was originally published under a pen name." *National Library of Scotland*, https://blog.nls.uk/sylvia-plaths-the-bell-jar-was-originally-published-under-a-pen-name/.

"Winter Care Tips for Fig Trees." *Lazy Dog Farm*, https://lazydogfarm.com/blogs/growing-figs/fig-tree-winter-care?srsltid=AfmBOoq80KCmC4jX-zKVhFm-LSJzfLkmRtO9ZDnaOkgN8q-mSuF7WVBtY.

"Phytalus." *My Eleusis*, https://myeleusis.com/en-us/the-myth/parallel-myths/phytalus/.

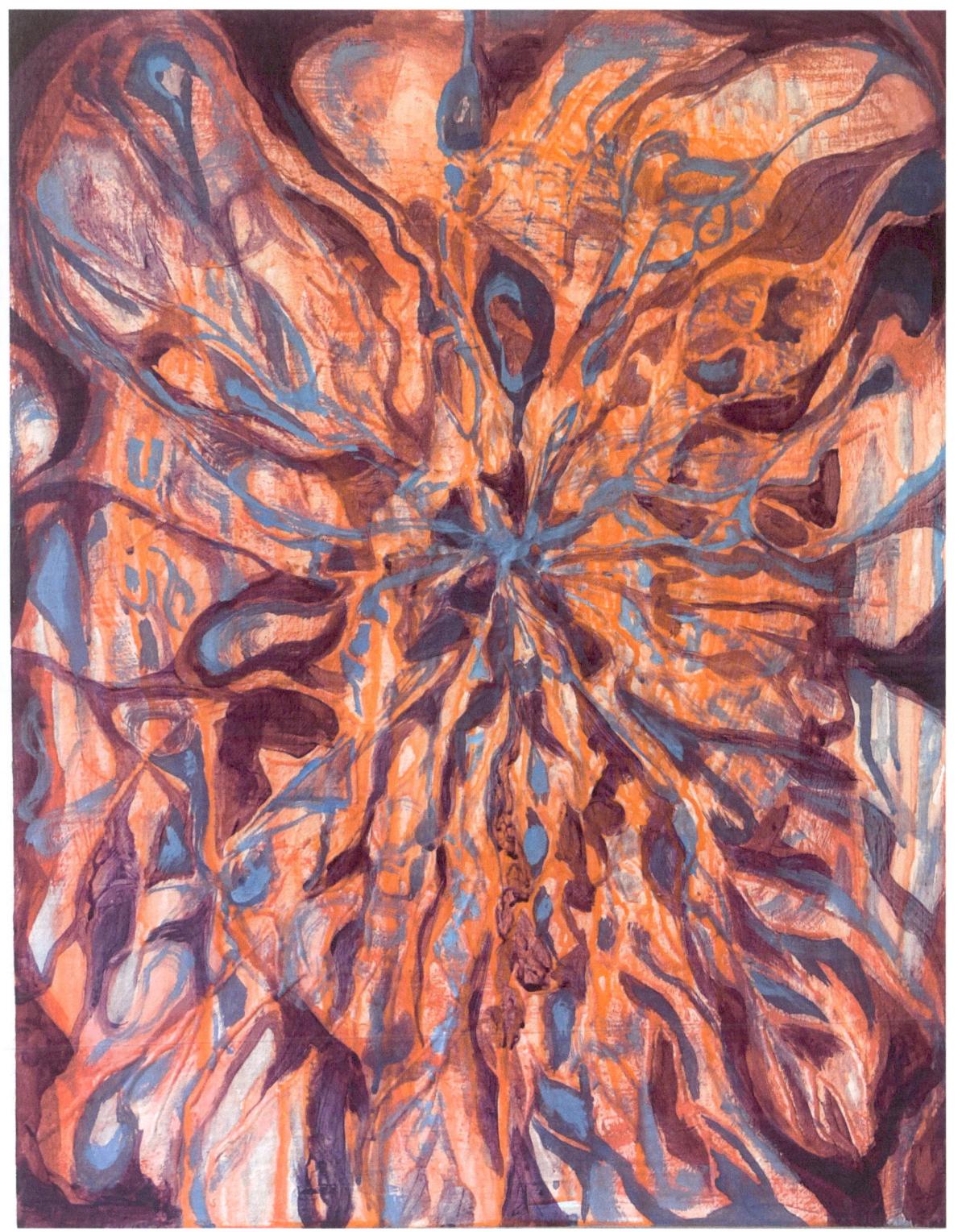

*Nervous Condition* (acrylic on wood panel), Emma Eager

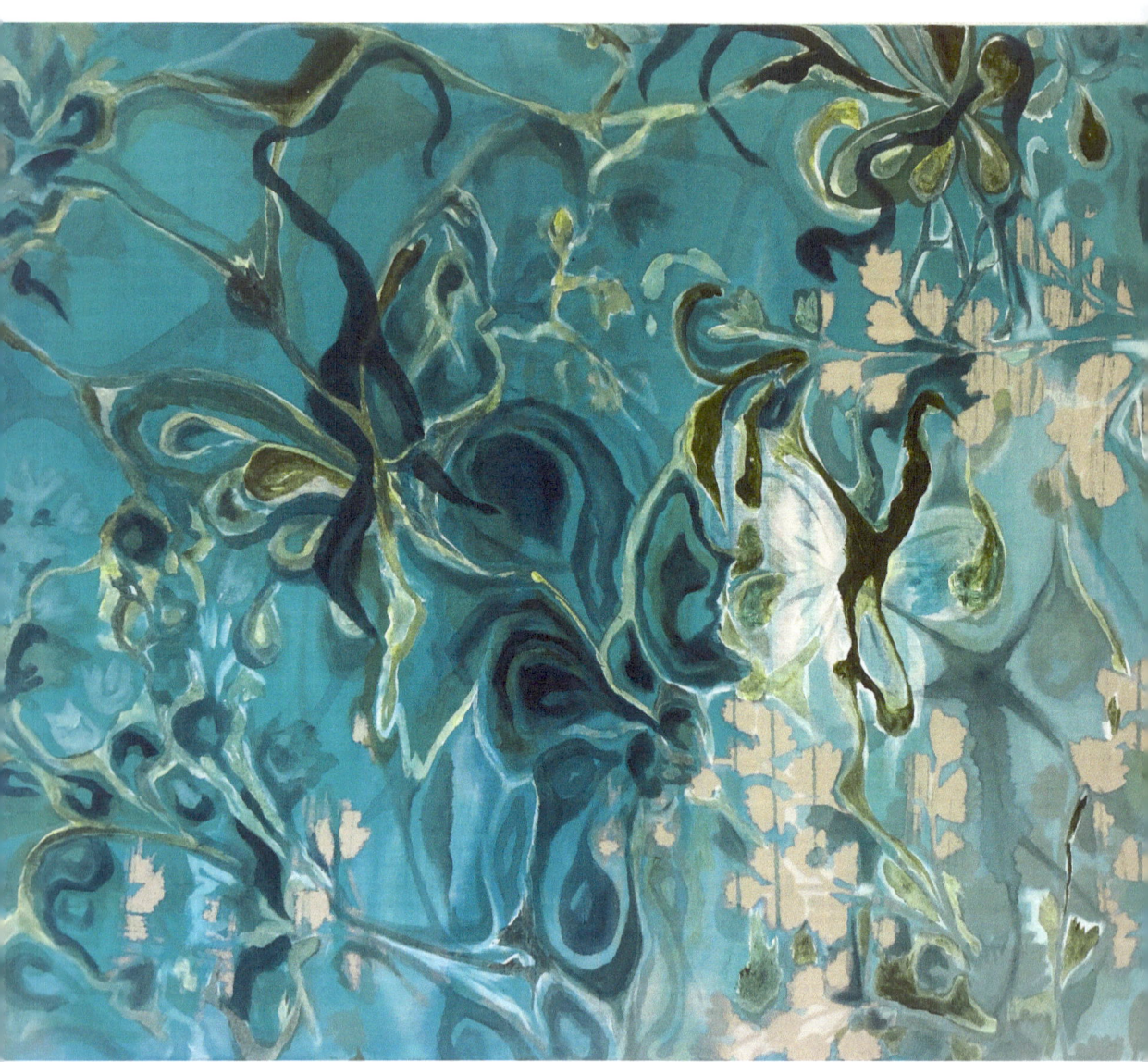

*Metamorphoses* (acrylic on cotton), Emma Eager

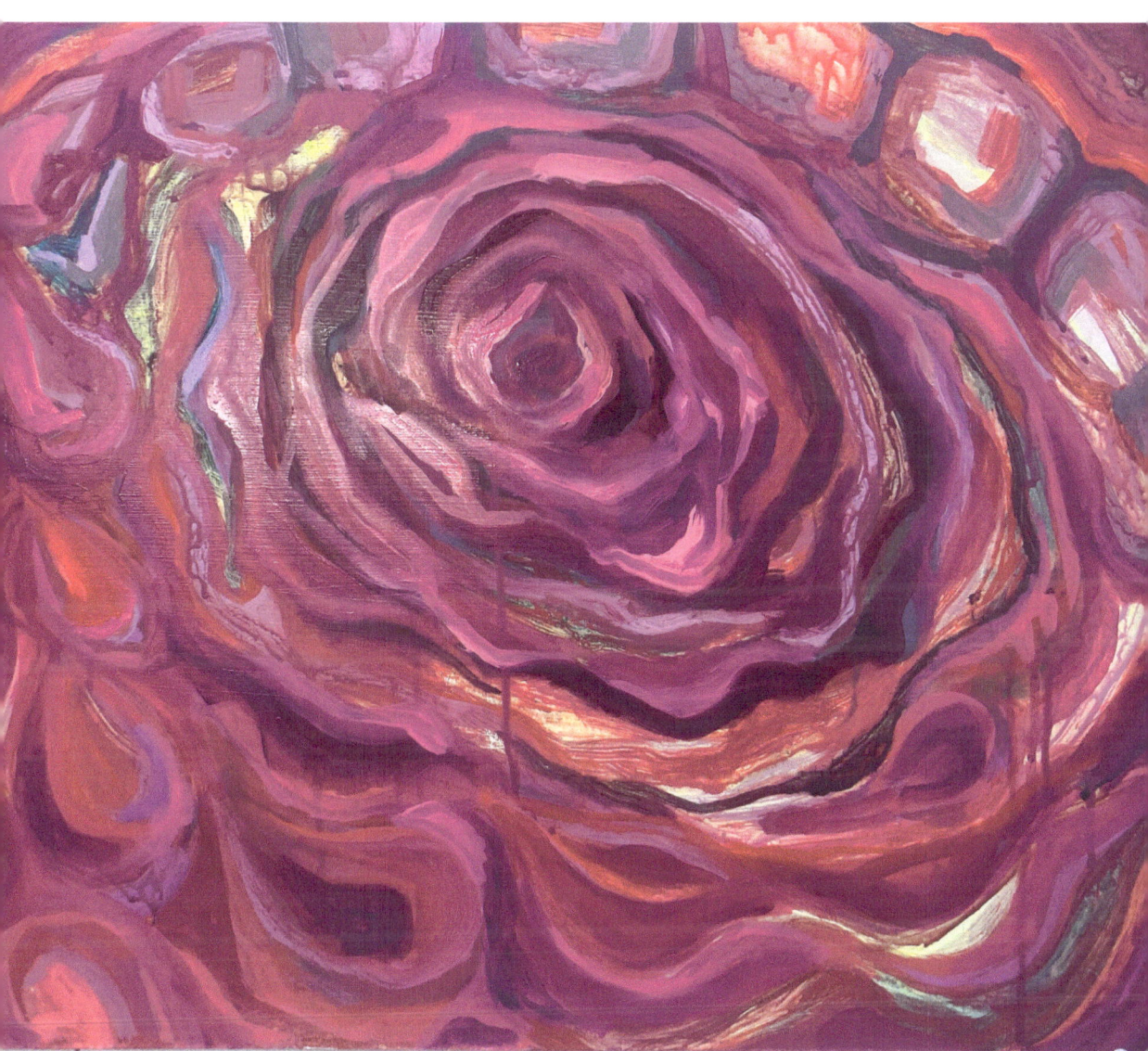

*Cavity* (oil on panel), Emma Eager

MONTY COOKE

# Zainab Abu Halib

Eyes clouded blue look
at a picture of a baby
who will never be a child.

Nursed by prayer in disaster—
an assertion that she could be.
Every breath a miracle,
every heartbeat stolen,
(surrounded by death himself.
Who was no god—
only a human man
with a stomach bloated by oil
and the slime of greed.)

Skin sunk behind
her eyelids
As receding muscle pulled hungrily
at her flesh,
begging for fat that isn't
there

The never child has a body
with a stomach bloated by her own emptiness
and dark eyes that would hold every star,
if they could see past five months old.

MONTY COOKE

# Elinguation

The tongue is mightier than the sword,
in sex and in war,
sink ships with tactful lips
if you know what you fight for.

Bite the hands that only feed
themselves
til their knuckles bleed
and their bones rebel.
Revel with outcasts on the margins
and let your music swell.

They'll try to smother
words that dance like flames,
as fire cannot be caged or tamed,
they'll spit their lies and shame.

But I'd rather my tongue
ripped from my throat,
than a pitiful corpse
of a torpid slug
decaying between my gums.

I won't tamper my fire,
won't let lyrics die unsung,
and if they steal them from my throat—
I'll hum.

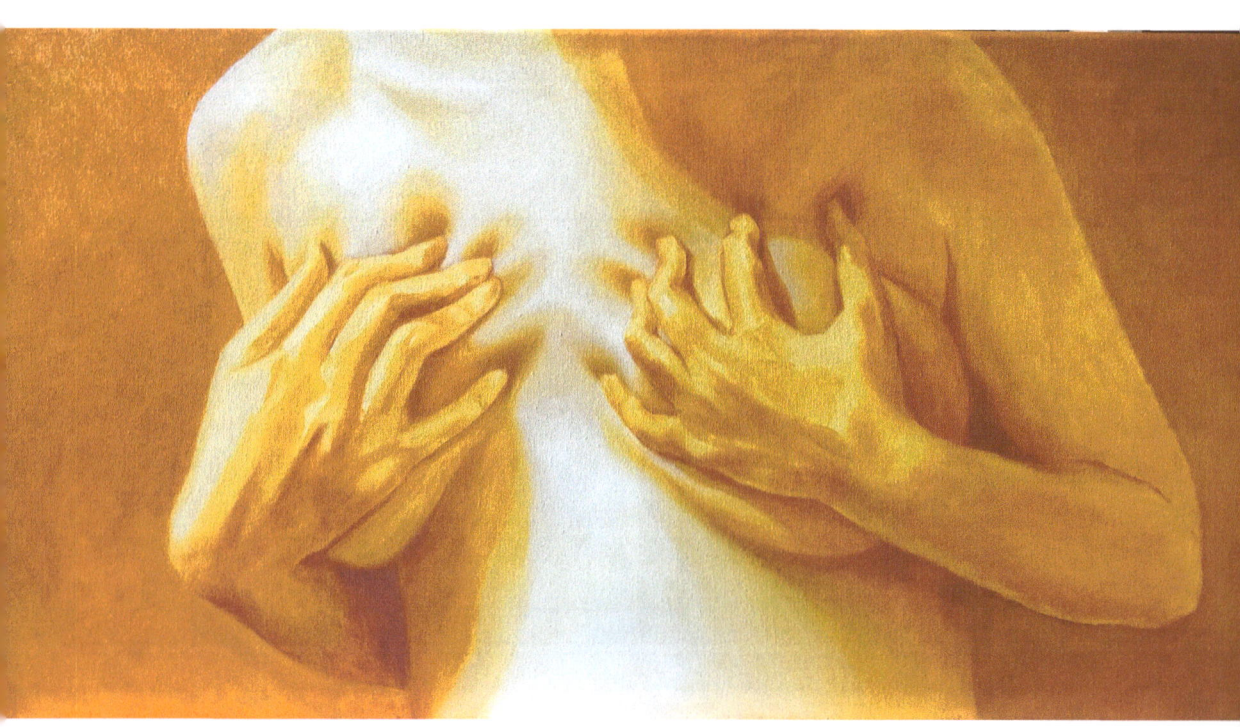

*Torment* (oil on canvas), Caitlin Andrejova

PAIGE LOUCKS

# *The Grand Scheme of Things*: A Review

Sarah Cedeño's debut collection, *The Grand Scheme of Things,* features twelve short stories connecting the lives of residents in Bridgeport, a fictional college town in Western New York. The characters range from toddlers to older couples, from college students to professors, all confronting grief, love, and the slow march of time. Despite only getting a glimpse into each character's life, readers can't help but feel intrinsically connected to every moment. In these stories of everyday life, Cedeño reveals her characters at their most vulnerable, while also framing them within the larger picture of human experience. She reminds us that while the pain is intimate, it is also entirely ordinary. In this way, she makes the entirety of Bridgeport feel real, as if we lived there too. The further the reader gets into the collection, the more genuine the fictional village becomes. Her stories, inspired by archival newspaper articles, span generations. This makes reading the collection feel like the stories are our own recollections of town gossip whispered around our kitchen table.

The collection begins with "The Wash," which focuses on a mother's most feared tragedy. Within a few paragraphs, we are blindsided just as Mabel is, as she learns the fate of her son Rusty who was accidentally drowned by Dakota, the neighbor's dog. Mabel recounts her grief in all of its frustrating, raw, and irrational glory. The use of a retrospective first-person narration allows Cedeño to provide a glimmer of hope even as we see Mabel in her darkest moments. As Mabel puts it, "when the impossible happens, you must accept it. Even if it runs like a spectacle around in your brain, or sits like a coal in your stomach, or severs the legs you once used to stand." This story sets the tone for the collection, giving readers a very clear depiction of both loss and acceptance. Mabel is not the first, nor will she be the last, to ever feel this way; however, her uniqueness comes from how she internalizes her grief and carries it with her. The story ends with Mabel and Dakota's owner, former adversaries, sharing a cigarette and watching their smoke dissipate.

Many of the stories collected here feature a looming figure in the background, a kind of threat that will upset the characters' lives as they know them. The threat might be the inevitable march of time, as in "House, History," where an older couple waits for the morning when their family home is to be bulldozed by the college. Other stories explore this idea more directly with the use of burglars, murderers, or other shady figures in the area. In "Dear Victor, If I Could Write You a Letter" the nameless narrator writes to Victor, insisting she wasn't trying to kiss him. She tells him about how she and Clara, his wife, decided that they were going to try and catch the Church Street Prowler, which becomes a way for the women to take hold of their own lives—and the burglar's escape pushes them further into their feelings of discontentment. At the end, the prowler haunts the narrator by standing and staring at her just long enough for her to imagine that he is Victor, and to think of what she might say to him.

One of my favorite aspects of this collection is how geographically connected the stories are. While characters from one story don't reappear in the others, many of them find importance in the same places. In "Professor Bird" we follow a college student at SUNY Bridgeport who is having an affair with her professor. At The Cellar, where they go for beers, they see a "Draft Beers Not Boys" sign. These reappear in the final story "Cold Storage," set during the Vietnam war. The way Cedeño intertwines the setting but not her characters encourages readers to wonder about the importance of the most significant moments of our lives. For example, in "Pooter from Church Street, circa 1990," Cedeño writes of a toddler who will soon be forgotten. The story begins with vivid descriptions of Pooter and his life: "Pooter was a chubby thumb of a toddler" and "The Purple house was occupied strictly by transients. Children ran in a never-ending supply around the front yard." It quickly changes pace to proclaim that despite these details, "No one remembered seeing Pooter writing on cracked sidewalks near the train tracks." Pooter becomes an idea, a vague memory to the residents of Church Street; they may remember that he existed but have forgotten everything that made him Pooter. Although that summer may have been the most remarkable of his life, to everyone else Pooter was just a neglected toddler who lived in the Purple House. In "Primal," the Purple House where he lived is again present, except this time it's dismissed as "the purple house, full of women with their young children." This repetition of place has the effect of revealing our alienation from our neighbors.

The collection ends with "Cold Storage," which wonderfully captures the complex feelings of anguish, freedom, and the self-absorption that comes with grieving. As the only novella in the collection, it allows us to sit longer with its characters. The reader feels the same aching pain that June and her mother do as they try to navigate their new lives. When June comes home from St. Barnabas Home for Unwed Mothers, having given birth to a daughter, she is confronted with her parent's divorce and the worsening of her mother's Multiple Sclerosis. The first-person narrative might have us empathize with June alone, but Cedeño reminds us that June's mother is also suffering, and that in fact, everyone has their own struggles. Of their separate battles, June says, "occasionally, we took turns crying. Neither of us had anything to offer as a consolation to the other. It was as though we were grieving something similar but in entirely different places." At the end, June goes home and sleeps, waiting for her mother to wake up so she can help take care of her. Ending this collection with a story of ambiguous loss reminds us of how complex grief can be, and because of this, shows us how crucial it is to find solace and community with the people close to us.

SONIA HOROWITZ

# An Interview with Sarah Cedeño

Sarah Cedeño is the author of *The Grand Scheme of Things*, her debut story collection published by Harbor Editions in July of 2025. She is also the author of a collection of essays titled, *Not Something We Discuss Often*. Cedeño teaches writing at her alma mater, SUNY Brockport, and also lives in Brockport with her husband, two sons, some old ghosts, and two German shepherds. Her work can be found in *Brevity*, *Salamander*, *The Journal*, *The Pinch*, *The Baltimore Review*, *Hippocampus Magazine*, *Bellevue Literary Review*, and elsewhere.

**Gandy Dancer: While reading** *The Grand Scheme of Things*, **I was struck by how personal and dark the collection felt, as there were a lot of themes about motherhood, death, and illness, with chronic illness being a major element of your previous collection of essays** *Not Something We Discuss Often*. **What experiences from your own life inspired you to write these stories and why did you feel like you needed to write this collection?**

Sarah Cedeño: I was spending a lot of time in the New York State digitized newspaper database researching the house we lived in at the time. Because I've always been a local history nerd, I became engrossed in the spectacles and everydayness in the *Brockport Republic/Democrat*. News stories served as an inspiration to explore the emotional sides of the articles to create characters. We don't always have historical journals to capture everyday lives, so I used newspapers to glimpse what life was like for residents at that time. A lot of the details in this collection were inspired by the advertisements, personal ads, images, and editorials surrounding the articles. And naturally, all that inspiration gets combined with my own curiosities, fears, memories, dreams, etc.

**GD: In the story, "Primal," you write, "children and parents were meant to live in separate worlds." In just one line, you break free from the common conception that a child naturally exists in their parent's world, as they were the one who granted them life and existence. I deeply admire how it recognizes the disjointed yet realness to familiar relationships, which is incorporated in some way in all of your stories. Why do you think it is important to examine these types of relationships, especially in fiction?**

SC: It was important to me to explore familial relationships because they are central to who we become, because we're all flawed and fine; because both parents and children are living their lives for the first time, and it can be hard to bridge an invisible gap. We are next to each other, regardless of age, but it's difficult amidst life's sometimes troubling circumstances, to remember those boundaries. In the generations that these stories take place, people weren't thinking so much about boundaries. As a child, Josie couldn't have fathomed how it would occur to Carla to know that her daughter was suicidal, and worse, to have her child's friend reveal this to her. I think these disconnects are worth trying to understand, however late, as Josie does in "Primal."

**GD: You use a number of different points of view and perspective across this collection. In "You Hear Night Sounds," Jimmy, the narrator, who grapples with his father dying from dementia, is in a second person point of view, which places us directly in the unbalanced and violent behavior he's experiencing. In "Professor Bird," Lottie, the protagonist, has an affair with her professor and is in a third person point of view, which allows us to question what motivates her need for validation from the patriarchy. How do you choose which point of view fits best for each story, and did you intentionally try to vary the perspectives in these stories?**

SC: I don't usually plan out the point of view, but with "You Hear Night Sounds," I wanted the unsettling impact the second person has on the narrative, to suggest the reader has entered Jimmy's mind, as "you." I'm most likely to default to a close third person when starting a story, and then that can change based on how the story develops. For example, "Dear Victor, If I Could Write You a Letter," eventually changed to first person because it took on the form of a letter. Lottie's narration, "In Professor Bird" stayed in a close third perspective. That closeness encourages the reader to slip into her experience.

**GD: The settings in *The Grand Scheme of Things* all take place in the fictional town of Bridgeport with references to real areas in Western New York such as the Erie Canal and many college campuses, like Bridgeport State Teacher's College, which I am assuming is in reference to SUNY Brockport's early**

name. When writing a story, is setting the initial thing you establish, and what drew you into writing a setting that is "close to home"?

SC: I think of setting as the threshold for readers to step into the story. Before I began the collection, I had decided to write a story cycle linked by place, a version of Brockport. I'm charmed and inspired by the village. When I found the digitized newspaper database (www.newyorkstatehistoricnewspapers.org), I spent hours exploring stories. It was a treasure trove of people and events.

**GD: I wasn't familiar with the phrase you use as your title. The protagonist of "The Wash" says "in the grand scheme of things, we are all harbingers of something." In this instance, she's tracing all the events that led up to her son's drowning in the canal. In that moment, she understands her own powerlessness. Many of your characters are in similar situations in which they come to terms with their own lack of power or agency to change the things that most trouble them. How did you choose this title and did it come before or after writing the collection?**

SC: The title didn't occur to me until the year before the book was published, several years after completing the first draft. My family was driving to a hockey game, and some minor "thing" became bigger than it needed to be, and I said, "In the grand scheme of things," and thought, Oh. That could be a title. It was universal and recognizable. The saying also implies that there is a grand scheme of things, and that we are all operators in that scheme.

**GD: You begin with an epigram from Alice Munro, who was recognized by the Nobel committee as a master of the contemporary short story. The quote reads, "Nobody knew the sober, victorious feeling she had sometimes, when she knew how much she was on her own." I admired how this quote related to a lot of the character's awareness of having to rely solely on themselves, even if that was what they needed or not. Did Munro's work inspire you while writing, and was this quote something you kept in mind while thinking about these stories?**

SC: I was reading a lot of Alice Munro during my MFA, while I was writing these stories. The richness of her stories, her focus on women's perspectives, and her inspiration from local history all inspired me. I didn't have the quote in mind as I wrote the stories, but came across it while re-reading, so I took it as kismet. I think a lot of the characters in the collection feel alone, maybe because they are coming to terms with life as an individual journey, which is especially difficult in the midst of societal and personal pressures or expectations.

**GD: I was pleased that the final story, "Cold Storage," was written as a novella, rather than a short story. The story is set during the Vietnam War, as teenage June leaves St. Barnabas, a home for unwed mothers. She considers returning to college, but instead returns home to divorced parents, and a**

mother who is dealing with Multiple Sclerosis. Can you talk about how this story came about? When did you know this would be a novella rather than a short story?

SC: I knew "Cold Storage" would be a novella rather than a short story because of the scope of the conflicts. There are several complex threads coalescing in June's life, and each complicates the others. I knew it would take space to tell the story. It was partly inspired by time I'd spent with my father researching rolls from the Catholic Charities when I was younger, trying to locate the child a family member had given up for adoption. I wanted to explore that complex loss and the disorienting setting of a Home for Unwed Mothers. I read a heartbreaking nonfiction book titled *The Girls Who Went Away* by Ann Fessler to get a sense of the experiences of women who were sent there. With June's mother, Alice, I wrote into my fears of what illness can do to the body, and how it can alter our lives profoundly and without warning.

**GD: The stories in this collection flowed into each other quite beautifully, and it didn't feel like there was any story that didn't earn its keep. How did you determine the order of these stories, and is that something you keep in mind while writing them?**

SC: There were many things I considered when ordering the stories—it's often suggested to put your strongest stories first. I thought "Cold Storage," the novella, was the strongest of all the pieces, but it felt strange to put a novella first, in my mind, too front-loaded. It made more sense at the end. I went with "The Wash" first. It was the first story I wrote for my MFA program, inspired by an article I discovered in which a dog named Idaho was put on trial for the murder of a 14-year-old boy. It was a huge news story at the time, in 1936, covered by the *New York Times* and Paramount Pictures's "The Eyes and Ears of the World." That the story was a real-life spectacle gave it the interest to put first. It's also the earliest, chronologically, so it set the feel of historical fiction, grounding the reader back in time. Beyond that, I considered the types of relationships featured in the stories. I considered length to balance the movement. There was a lot of switching around! To make the process simpler, I printed versions of the stories for easy access to content, stapled them individually, and laid them out on the floor, rearranging them as I made decisions.

**GD: I had the opportunity to meet you in person and was inspired by how you described your writing process. What advice would you give to someone who is interested in writing a short story collection?**

SC: Read a lot of story collections. Be open to the world. Seek and hoard what's interesting to you. Be stubborn in the interest of your characters—give them their epiphanies. Have fun. Tear a story apart and put it back together (save all drafts). Distill your writing by cutting the word count of your stories as much as you can. Trust the process.

POSTSCRIPT                                          JESSE CURRAN

# Seagull Motif (Violet and Green)

*—Arthur Dove, 1928*

From the deck of the yawl, he stares at the spit of land the locals call Sand City. He fixes his gaze on a single seagull, in motion against a seascape of sunset. He sees the line she shapes long before fancy cameras might lapse time or layer exposure upon exposure upon exposure so that the slow-eyed human might better behold the startling swoops of a flock of starlings. Instead, he wields the brush, tracing the figure eight ribbon she unfolds as she glides. He wants to get closer to the sensation of flight. He wants to find ways to use paint to extract the essence of the bird whose element is all edge effect, a creature who moves between land and sea and earth and sky. Her path figures and shapes and seeks fodder. And because it's the twenties and the yawl is his home, he likely has the phonograph cranked so that the Gershwin is also part of the scene, another course in the bounty of sensation. There's rhythm in the light and on the beach and in the sea. There's the seagull being a seagull. There's the gall of a gull to consider landing on the deck of a yawl to swipe a bit of his sandwich before she lifts off once more. Wings like propellers, an instinctual physics of lift and thrust. Resting on airs that push up and riding the thermals that ascend from the bay. He's not worried so much about how they fly, just glad that they do. That they do in a world of sink and submersion. He's a sailor, after all, another being who can sense the southwesterly on a cellular level. For a moment, he dwells in the ancient longing to shuck his humanness for an avian being ever knowing he can't. His wings are the sails, his flight is to paint. His work is to behold the lift and glide and to hear its music and then to make the music something we might see, knowing all of this is a bit more than a metaphor. He drifts with the bay's currents. The boat rises and falls with the wind and the sea. The bands of radiant light; the colors of concentricity; the conical swirling of clouds; the bird's motif, her motive, her motion. Both his eyes and the gull's find ways to flush out the salt so they might keep seeing. Who knows if she can see color, but he can see her plumage, how gray and black make green. How the clouds tear open, how gray and blue make violet. And how on this stretch of sand, the jingle shells lend a peach glow, the mother-of-pearl layer where the gull searches for stray mollusks. From the deck of a yawl, gazing at the spit of land, he puts oil on metal, knowing the motif is what impels, what guides, what awakens. The seagull's motif is the force line of her flight, and she sets his paintbrush in motion.

POSTSCRIPT                                                       JESSE CURRAN

# "Landscape at Cagnes"

*—Arthur Dove, 1908*

This is over there. Sun-drenched, lemon trees, skies like birds' eggs,
groves mint green, paint daubed and lush with summer plums

a hill town hugged between Antibes and Nice before the beaches
became famed for expat summer *fêtes* fueled by martinis and mayhem.

This is over there, old villas, white stone gleaming back ten centuries
of sun, one of a dozen landscapes you did of *le Midi*. Most were lost.

You left that style there, along with a painting of a lobster
and a still life with a bowl of fruit and flowery wallpaper.

You left Monet and Renoir and took back a tiny bit of Matisse.
You packed in your trunk a stack of canvases, the famed Kandinsky book

and came back here to the streets of Manhattan, to the Long Island Sound.
You came back to engine grease under your nails and photo chemicals in your nose

and skyscraper construction in your eyes and Gershwin in your ears
and to a palette without pastels, exchanging birds' eggs for metallic steel.

You came back to oak tree bark, thunderstorms, derricks, and ferries,
back to transcendentalists who thought God was nature and so are we.

You came here to this harbor, to where I now feel settled, mortgaged, seasoned
tending to pear trees and admitting kids don't easily fly across an ocean.

You were content to leave it, a scene you never needed, a son of upstate,
the Finger Lakes, the Catskills between, Islands of Manhattan and Paumanok.

This is the painting that shows you knew your stuff.
Everything that followed showed how you made it new.

POSTSCRIPT

JESSE CURRAN

# "Partly Cloudy"

*—Arthur Dove, 1942*

He was a watcher of weather, a captain of winds.
A surveyor of atmospheric wanderings. His hair
and eyes taste like the sea from a swim in the sound
and from fresh-caught flounder for dinner.
He sees the second the tide shifts, ruminates
on the patterns in the cosmos, quivers
with the wild currents swelling round us.
Partly cloudy is both forecast and drama,
great beasts of magic swiftly streaming
across the heavens. And the sun, worthy
of worship, even in the roaring twenties,
even with cars and skyscrapers and machines
making sails and the gales that animate them
less needed. Somehow, it's all connected—
circle circling circle, held high in the center,
energy undulating out, passing through the clouds
and the sky and then into my circular eyes
just like the jazz notes swim in his cells
and the swimmer shapes a sun with her arms
and the ripples reach me, volts of ancient electricity.
There's so much in this world we might only see
when we stop and watch how the wind shifts
through it. He chose the space between two necks,
which means he chose the place that in turn
chose me, and I choose partly cloudy days

for all the unexpected ways they have me
watching, witnessing, wondering
how to bridge this space between us.
Clouds like kidney beans jigging and jiggering
to his mandolin. A forecast straight from heaven,
a sense that all is change, and, with eyes on the skies,
all is right.

# About the Authors

CAITLIN ANDREJOVA is a Central New York artist who specializes in oil painting and graphite artwork. Using figural expressions, she focuses on themes of love, appreciation, comfort, and their opposites such as grief, depression, and anger. She has received an Associate's Degree in illustration from Mohawk Valley Community College, a Bachelor's Degree in Fine Arts (drawing and painting) from SUNY New Paltz, and is currently pursuing her Master's of Fine Arts in studio art at University at Buffalo.

NOAH BANAS is a junior majoring in English at SUNY Geneseo.

PAULINA BARGNESI is pursuing her BA in English and media studies at University of Buffalo. She is unable to write without music and often finds that her head goes far too fast for her pen.

SAM CARRILLO is studying computer science at the SUNY at Buffalo. He serves as the secretary of the University at Buffalo's Poetry Club, where he devotes himself wholeheartedly to the creative act of writing.

MICHAELA CHITTENDEN is an artist who blends historical themes with story-driven imagery. Her work often reflects on identity and storytelling and connects the past and the present. She's loved art for as long as she can remember, and spends her time sketching, planning, and experimenting with ways to make history feel alive on the page. When she's not creating, you can find her writing, playing violin, researching, or daydreaming.

MONTY COOKE (they/he) is an English adolescent education major at SUNY Fredonia. They often host open mics in their hometown and are the events coordinator for SUNY Fredonia's Writers' Ring. Monty's work has been published in the 2024 and 2025 edition of *The Trident*, Fredonia's literary magazine.

MICHAEL CROWLEY is an undergrad at SUNY Geneseo from Eden, NY, studying English (literature) and philosophy. In his spare time, he enjoys reading, writing poetry, gardening, spending time in parks, snowboarding, and most other outdoor activities.

JESSE CURRAN is a poet, essayist, scholar, and teacher who lives in Northport, NY. Her essays and poems have appeared in dozens of literary journals including *After the Art, Literary Mama, About Place*, and *The Denver Quarterly*. She is the 2025 Long Island Poet of the Year and Assistant Professor in the Department of English at SUNY Old Westbury. www.jesseleecurran.com

JENNA CURTIS is from Rochester, NY and attends SUNY Oswego, where she is studying adolescent education and creative writing. When she is not studying or working, she loves to spend her free time reading and writing with a cup of iced coffee in her hand or buttered popcorn by her side. You can find her work in SUNY Oswego's *Great Lake Review* and *Gandy Dancer 13.2*.

REY DAVIS is a freshman at Stony Brook University, majoring in creative writing. They write poems, flash fiction, and creative nonfiction. Recently, they began sharing their poetry on social media and hope to pursue a career in editing and publishing in the future.

ALYSSA DAWSON is a hobbyist writer and a professional *New York Times* crossword puzzle enjoyer. She is also a second-year political science and international relations major at SUNY Geneseo. In her free time, she enjoys painting, watching movies, and talking incessantly about her niche interests.

DAN OWEN DE VERA is a freshman at SUNY University at Buffalo, where he is studying computer science.

EMMA EAGER is a senior at SUNY Purchase, where she is a dual degree student in painting and literature alongside a minor in art history. In her copious free time, she enjoys cooking, baking, and crocheting sweaters for her cat. Emma's work has appeared in Purchase's *Sub Mag* and *Italics Mine*, the latter of which featured her work as the cover of Issue 20.

BELLE ELYSE is a junior at SUNY Purchase, where they are pursuing a degree in creative writing. This is their first publication. They are currently in your closet or under your bed.

GABRIELLA FERRI is a full-time student studying sustainability at SUNY Delhi. In her free time, she enjoys painting, illustration, and photography.

MAX FLANIGAN is a senior fine arts student attending the University at Buffalo. He is a visual artist focused on abstract imagery. Often his work deals with issues such as technological advancement, industrialism, and humanity in the modern era. Recently he has been focusing on the visual language used by low-cost construction and efficient infrastructure–grids, lines, squares, and other basic shapes. He is interested in how our society is made up of these shapes, which contribute to feelings of isolation and disconnect.

GIULYANA GAMERO is a senior communication major at SUNY Geneseo and the former Youth Poet for the city of Rockford. She loves to take on artistic projects in any medium, such as 89.3 WGSU's Sunflower Story Hour, a paranormal audio drama. Her writing has appeared in *Gandy Dancer* issue 13.1, *Young American Poetry Digest*, *The Lamron*, and in Carnegie Hall's Traveling the Spaceways. Her visual art has appeared at the Rockford Art Museum and Bridgeport Art Center.

ABIGAIL HALBERT is a junior at SUNY Fredonia, where she studies English and creative writing. When she isn't doing coursework, she enjoys playing D&D and writing short fiction.

Monica Hejaily is a first-year student at SUNY Geneseo, where she is studying English and adolescence education. She has enjoyed art her whole life, with a special love for acrylic painting over the past few years.

Kira Hook is a New York-based writer and creative writing student at Stony Brook University. Her flash fiction has been featured at multiple showcases, including the 2025 Shirley Strum Kenney Arts Festival.

Jasmeen Kaur is a student at SUNY Old Westbury studying computer science. She has taken classes in creative writing and poetry writing. Her poetry explores memory, identity, and the natural world through vivid imagery and emotional reflection. She draws inspiration from everyday places and moments of stillness. Her poetry has been shaped by voices like Ada Limón and Ocean Vuong, blending tenderness with strength and clarity.

Buzz Kozak is a senior at Purchase College studying playwriting. When not writing for the stage, he writes poetry, which has previously appeared in *Dadakuku*.

Archer Maduro is a senior at SUNY Geneseo, studying English (creative writing). With a long-term dream of working in editing and publishing, they primarily write creative nonfiction and poetry. Archer has been previously published in *Gandy Dancer* and Geneseo's *Iris Magazine*.

Jade Maracic is a 21-year-old artist earning her BFA at the Fashion Institute of Technology. Working primarily in oil paint, her practice centers on capturing the nuances of human experience through observation and emotional depth. Her work reflects a deep interest in the everyday moments, gestures, and expressions that reveal our shared humanity. Her work appears in *Gandy Dancer* 13.2.

Ana Paul is a singer-songwriter based in both Port Washington and Buffalo, New York. She continues to work on her music while pursuing a college degree in psychology. Ana also founded the Undergraduate Poetry Club at the University at Buffalo and has hosted various readings throughout Buffalo. She is in continuous exploration of her childhood passions—singing, writing, painting, and exploring the realms of this realm.

Owen Penhollow is a junior at the University at Buffalo studying economics, philosophy, political science, and mathematics. He writes things that make him giggle at least once. Sometimes they are also meaningful (albeit rarely). In his free time, he enjoys self-deprecating humor and malapropisms.

Stephen Piazza is an English major at SUNY Albany from Mount Kisco, New York. His work has previously been featured in *ARCH* magazine and will be performed at the University's 2025 annual student play festival.

Sawyer Taylor Ramsamooj, a student at SUNY Fashion Institute of Technology studying fine arts, is a mixed media artist. She labels herself an abstract expressionist, relying on her feelings to create movement on a canvas. She derives inspiration from music, emotions, and colors in nature. One of her favorite works is a piece called "Los Moscos" by Mark Bradford.

KATERINA RONCONI is an emerging writer, pursuing her undergraduate degree in Stony Brook's Creative Writing BFA program. Born in Italy and raised in New York City, her fiction interweaves the diverse aesthetics and daily realities of the city with her own personal experiences of disjointedness, crafting tales that mine the leftovers of people. Raw and unflinching, she toys with the notion of civility and sanctimony deep-seated in all of us.

VICTORIA STIVER is a senior at SUNY New Paltz, currently studying for a BFA in painting and drawing. Most familiar with traditional methods of painting and drawing, Stiver has been expanding her use of unconventional and mixed mediums over the past several months in order to explore themes more profoundly through form and materiality. Her work has been published in *Assembly Art Journal*, the SUNY New Paltz student-led online magazine.

NATALIE VAZQUEZ-MARTINEZ is a senior at SUNY Plattsburgh, pursuing a BA in Art. As an artist, she works with vibrant colors and diverse textures across multiple media, with a primary focus on oil painting. She is interested in exploring how texture and color in art can communicate sensory experiences for individuals who aren't neurotypical.

SHEILA VERKAIK (she/they/he) is a four-thyear student of modern history and creative writing at SUNY Purchase. Originally from Harlem, their work is often inspired by their New York City upbringing, the world around them, and the past. Recently, Sheila has been taking an interest in her Dutch heritage and citizenship and has endeavored to start learning Dutch. Upon graduation, he hopes to continue his education in the Netherlands.

SHADAE WALKER is a sophomore at SUNY Delhi, a multidisciplinary artist and emerging architect whose work is shaped by emotion as much as design. Blending structure with soul, she layers faces, symbols, and space to explore themes of rebirth, faith, and the balance between strength and softness. Each piece reflects a process of becoming a reconstruction of self and spirit. Through her art, Walker transforms vulnerability into form and turns personal pain into something powerful, intentional, and beautifully alive.

LORI YAMOND is a junior at SUNY Old Westbury, where she is studying multicultural English literature and foundations of creative writing. In her free time, she enjoys reading, writing, crocheting and managing the Little Free Library she owns in her hometown.

www.ingramcontent.com/pod-product-compliance
Lightning Source LLC
Chambersburg PA
CBHW051912210526
45473CB00006B/1982